Playwork in Practice

ALSO AVAILABLE FROM BLOOMSBURY

Early Childhood Theories and Contemporary Issues, Mine Conkbayir and Christine Pascal

Early Childhood and Neuroscience, Mine Conkbayir

Critical Childhood Studies, E. Kay M. Tisdall, John M. Davis, Deborah Fry, Kristina Konstantoni, Marlies Kustatscher, M. Catherine Maternowska and Laura Weiner

Reflective Teaching in Early Education, Jennifer Colwell and Amanda Ince with Helen Bradford, Helen Edwards, Julian Grenier, Eleanor Kitto, Eunice Lumsden, Catriona McDonald, Juliet Mickelburgh, Mary Moloney, Sheila Nutkins, Ioanna Palaiologou, Deborah Price and Rebecca Swindells

Ethics and Research with Young Children, edited by Christopher M. Schulte

Creativity and Making in Early Childhood, Mona Sakr, Bindu Trivedy, Nichola Hall, Laura O'Brien and Roberto Federici

Playwork in Practice

Applying the Playwork Lens Across the Children's Workforce

Ali Wood, Julia Sexton and Jacky Kilvington

BLOOMSBURY ACADEMIC
LONDON • NEW YORK • OXFORD • NEW DELHI • SYDNEY

BLOOMSBURY ACADEMIC
Bloomsbury Publishing Plc
50 Bedford Square, London, WC1B 3DP, UK
1385 Broadway, New York, NY 10018, USA
29 Earlsfort Terrace, Dublin 2, Ireland

BLOOMSBURY, BLOOMSBURY ACADEMIC and the Diana logo are trademarks of Bloomsbury Publishing Plc

First published in Great Britain 2024

Copyright © Ali Wood, Julia Sexton and Jacky Kilvington, 2024

Ali Wood, Julia Sexton and Jacky Kilvington have asserted their right under the Copyright, Designs and Patents Act, 1988, to be identified as Authors of this work.

For legal purposes the Acknowledgements on p. x constitute an extension of this copyright page.

Cover design by Grace Ridge
Cover image © Zing Images / Getty Images

All rights reserved. No part of this publication may be reproduced or transmitted in any form or by any means, electronic or mechanical, including photocopying, recording, or any information storage or retrieval system, without prior permission in writing from the publishers.

Bloomsbury Publishing Plc does not have any control over, or responsibility for, any third-party websites referred to or in this book. All internet addresses given in this book were correct at the time of going to press. The author and publisher regret any inconvenience caused if addresses have changed or sites have ceased to exist, but can accept no responsibility for any such changes.

A catalogue record for this book is available from the British Library.

A catalog record for this book is available from the Library of Congress.

ISBN: HB: 978-1-3501-6202-0
PB: 978-1-3501-6201-3
ePDF: 978-1-3501-6203-7
eBook: 978-1-3501-6204-4

Typeset by Deanta Global Publishing Services, Chennai, India
Printed and bound in Great Britain

To find out more about our authors and books visit www.bloomsbury.com and sign up for our newsletters.

We would like to dedicate this book to all those who work across the children's workforce who recognize and understand children and young people's need and right to play – they have our deepest admiration for swimming against the tide and supporting and advocating for children and young people in their workplaces and elsewhere.

Contents

List of Figures viii
Preface ix
Acknowledgements x

1 **Play and Playwork** 1

2 **Behaviour and Adult Expectations** 21

3 **Education** 37

4 **Inclusion** 55

5 **Space, Environment and the Outdoors** 69

6 **Age, Risk and Resilience** 87

7 **Emotions and Resilience** 101

8 **Health and Well-being** 119

9 **Gender** 135

Afterword 153

Appendix 155
References 161
Index 184

Figures

1.1 Chasing robots 14
2.1 I'm not obviously watching you (but I'm here) 24
3.1 Making your own space at school matters 47
4.1 Wall story 61
5.1 Me and my friends go under the coats 71
5.2 Toys on the ledge 82
5.3 Monster game 84
6.1 Easy when you know how 92
7.1 Will I make it? 102
7.2 Socio-ecological model 112
8.1 Playing Basecamp 126
8.2 Playing Basecamp undercover 128
9.1 Role reversal? 136
A3.1 Risk/Benefit Assessment Form 160

Preface

We – Julia, Ali and Jacky – had not written as a threesome before, so we set out originally to meet up regularly to co-create this work, chapter by chapter, and to share ideas and experiences and stories that illustrate how to use the playwork approach in many different settings. We had not long begun when the Covid-19 pandemic also began, and the impact of this on each of our lives in terms of general well-being, illnesses and family bereavements, as well as not being able to meet face to face, has meant we have had to operate differently with each of us writing separate chapters and then trying to critically weave these together to make a whole. It has therefore not been quite the 'meshwork of entangled lines of life, growth and movement' (Ingold 2011:63) we intended, and the writing experience has been a little lonelier. But we met up on Zoom from time to time in order to still maximize what we could learn and gain from each other's knowledge and experience about play and the practice of playwork and to create conditions that might support playfulness (Lester 2020) – just as essential for writing as for playing. We hope that we have still done our subject justice and enabled our readers across the children's workforce to catch the essence of play in children's lives, how we can all support it and why we absolutely should. To those of you working with children in education, hospitals, youth services, prisons, sport, foster care and childcare, and those of you with parent and carer responsibilities, who shared your stories with us, we thank you – keep playing!

Acknowledgements

We would particularly like to thank all the wonderful individuals who gave us both their time and their stories.

1
Play and Playwork

Chapter Outline

Play as an outcome
Play as intrinsically motivated behaviour
Play and playwork value
Risk in play
Playworkers as reflexive reflectors
State of unknowingness/Negative capability
Adulteration
The playwork approach

The following eight characteristics neatly summarize the underpinning philosophy of playwork that enables playworkers to practise in a way that they believe benefits children rather than adult's conceptualisations of children.

- A conceptualization of the child that actively resists dominant and subordinating narratives and practices
- A belief that while playing, the 'being' child is far more important than the 'becoming' child
- An adherence to the principle that the vital outcomes of playing are derived by children in inverse proportion to the degree of adult involvement in the process
- A non-judgemental acceptance of the children as they really are, running hand in hand with an attitude, when relating to the children, of 'unconditional positive regard'

- An approach to practice that involves a willingness to relinquish adult power, suspend any preconceptions and work to the children's agenda
- The provision of environments that are characterized by flexibility, so that the children are able to create (and possibly destroy and re-create) their own play environments according to their own needs
- A general acceptance that risky play can be beneficial, and that intervention is not necessary unless a safety or safeguarding issue arises
- A continuous commitment to deep personal reflection that manages the internal relationship between their present and former child-self, and the effects of that relationship on their current practice (Brown, Long and Wragg 2018:717).

This chapter will look at 'playwork as practice' rather than 'playwork in practice'. We and other playwork authors (Brown, Long and Wragg 2018, Lester, Russell and Smith 2017, Lester 2020, King and Newstead 2018) understand playwork as a form of ongoing research (rather like play itself) – playworkers constantly paying attention to what is going on where and when children are playing; reflecting on this and trying to work out how best to support a playful atmosphere that will lead to more playing for play's own sake and not for any instrumental purposes. What we mean by this, simply put in the words of Brown (2008:8), is that 'the first aim of playworkers is to create a rich play environment that enables play to take place'. Lester (2020) suggests that playworkers create 'spheres of possibility' where anything can happen or a 'play saturated atmosphere' where, in the words of Guilbaud (2018:119), playworkers can 'be altered by what is happening, as opposed to being, by our own perceptions, its shaping influence'. This is no easy task given the prevailing discourse in the West regarding children as inferior to adults in some way (Wragg 2018), where it would be accepted that any adult working with children should be in charge and responsible for organizing and managing a finished environment for children to play in, in such a way that the children's play behaviours could be anticipated by the workers as leading to some sort of developmental outcome. 'Most adults who are in contact with children bring their own agenda to the relationship. The playworker is unusual in as much as s/he attempts to suspend all personal prejudice and go along with the flow of children's needs and tastes' (Brown 2008:10).

Anybody who has ever truly observed children at play, trying to see from a child's perspective (we will say more about this), without an adult taking the role of the person designated as 'in charge', or being oppressive by their presence, will know that unexpected things happen, which are completely acceptable, even desirable, within a playwork approach. It is inappropriate to try and anticipate what will be experienced and to try and judge what the outcomes might be, apart from perhaps for the child or children to have enjoyed playing and feeling more alive. When playing, children are political actors or activists (Lester and Russell 2013, 2014) changing, or trying to change, the world to suit their own notions; to make their own decisions; to push boundaries; to create and break rules to choose sides and so on. They do not play to develop, although they may inadvertently develop or as Russell and Lester (2013) suggest 'emerge' or 'become' or 'be', through their play.

Example
To provide a nice, welcoming environment, a little snuggle area, with rug, cushions and a blanket, had been created by her mum, in Jacky's two-year-old granddaughter Ava's somewhat stark new bedroom in the house her family had just moved into, moving her from her previous cozy small bedroom. On one side, there was a small box with books and on the other side, a small box with assorted toys. At first sight, during the afternoon, Ava lay down, pulled the blanket over her, and said, 'night-night'. Jacky said 'night-night', turned off the light and went out of the room. After a moment, Ava called out 'morning time' and Jacky went back into the room and turned the light on saying 'morning, did you sleep well?' as Ava sat up and then got up laughing. This was repeated over and over with much hilarity. Further games of going to bed were enacted with a tiny model cat whose home was the tiniest stacking block hidden behind a cushion. 'Where's cat?' Ava would say, and Jacky would look for the cat by looking behind and in various things until she found the cat in a cube and would say 'here's cat'. Ava would say 'cat's bed, cat's home'. Ava's slightly larger model cat became involved, and its home was a larger cube, but Jacky was not supposed to hunt for it. When Jacky moved cushions to look for the larger cat, Ava said 'No' and put the cushions back. It merely got hidden behind a cushion and was looked at periodically by Ava. Nothing was said about it. It was just looked at. This was repeated until tea was ready.

During the period of play with Ava, Jacky was present and participating but was not in charge of the playing. The playing was chosen by Ava, it unfolded under her direction; it continued for the time that she chose (teatime excepted); it changed when she chose to change it and it came from her imagination. Jacky played along or what in playwork might be termed 'engaged in simple involvement' or 'intervened in an un-adulterating way'. Playworkers see the intrinsic value of play for its own sake with no accompanying decided purpose or outcome because the child wants to play and because playing leads to more playing which is vitally important in the life of a child. Other professionals may be more interested in the instrumental aspects of play to promote certain areas of development and well-being, as an aid to learning or the development of physical, cognitive, social and emotional skills.

We could reflect on this example from different perspectives. A non-directive therapist might interpret Ava's play behaviour, post playing, as therapeutic play, with Ava acting out rituals of bedtime and waking in a strange environment to feel a sense of normality about it and not be scared; being in an obscure place and feeling more hidden than in her previous very small bedroom but being 'found' in there. If we focused on play's role in children's emotional development, the therapeutic benefits of Ava's play behaviour might be identified, or her play could be viewed as future-focused, as she might be practising being a grown-up. From a gender point of view, Ava had clearly been provided with a culturally and socially typical environment for girls within which to play and she played in a stereotypical way that might be expected from girls in much of society – she was not boisterous; she was nurturing and caring. From an educational point of view, Ava may have been involved in a containment schema – which size cat fitted into which size cube? A parent, or early years practitioner, with educational expectations may have tried to develop the game by asking questions or putting their own ideas into the game to use it as a learning opportunity for Ava. This type of scaffolding has become a key concept in play-based learning, when an adult intervenes, albeit in a gentle way, to develop a child's playing towards an early learning goal.

Any number of close analyses may unravel a host of different interpretations. Whatever the reason for playing, Ava did play in the way that she played. If left to her own devices, anything could have been played at that Ava wanted to play and, in any way, that she wanted to play. The catalyst for the playing was initially the amalgamation of rug, cushions and blanket with some other resources, for example, books and toys available and granny, which was a new 'sphere of possibility' Lester (2020: 23) for Ava. Jacky, in her role as granny, and using her playworker experience, was able to, in the words of Lester (2020:87) 'co-create the playful atmosphere where adults and children can get on and go on together'.

Lester (2020:85) speaks of 'playspacetimes' (which will be further explored in Chapter 5), a place that has a 'distinctive affective register of pleasure, nonsense, uncertainty and unpredictability' (ibid:88) and the cosy snuggle area fulfilled these qualities at this time. Hughes (2018:209) terms this a 'moment by moment amalgamation, both visible and invisible of these changing influences', which involves discrete play behaviour, particular mind-sets (adult and child) and a mix of place, space and time and everything within these. The same place, same things, same bodies, at another time might become entangled in a different way to form a different playful expression. Play is not predictable, it is 'quixotic (unpredictable, fanciful), emergent, indeterminate, spontaneous, improvised and so on' (Lester 2020:200) and thus adults planning for play is like planning for a specific number of birds to sing in the trees at dawn.

From the above, by no means exhaustive thoughts on how Ava's playing might be perceived; we can see that there are many ways of thinking about play which, as Sutton-Smith (2009) says, leads to its ambiguity, which also 'produces key challenges for its recognition and status' (Cullen and Johnston 2018:5). Because play and playing are an important focus of playwork, it seems that 'such ambiguity of purpose (can) lead experts in play to have a less serious, established and recognized status amongst other professionals' (ibid:3). Playworkers specialize in play to support children in their playing, whatever their circumstances and in whatever way they choose to play. Professionals in other spheres support play for other important purposes because they recognize the importance of play, but not to merely support the playing child to play or play more. For instance, early years workers support play to help children to develop aspects of themselves such as their sociability and their physical and creative ability (Bruce 2011a). Play therapists support play to assist children in healing themselves and to overcome traumas (Webb 2015). Schools allow play in break times so that children can let off steam after periods of concentration and be ready to concentrate again (Pellegrini 2005). Uniformed group leaders support play to help with team building (Dégi and Asztalos 2021). Sports coaches support play to help children find fun and freedom in sports. Tom Hartley (2023) says 'Play is the invisible thread weaving together creativity, learning, and joy, ultimately transforming the tapestry of athletic development into a masterpiece of skill and passion'. We fervently believe in the importance of children's play for its own sake and the importance of the playwork approach to the lives of children, and in this book, we explore some of the different perspectives in relation to adult–child relationships that are manifested because of the different 'uses' of play. We shall consider the potential meaning behind interactions that fall within different perspectives and hopefully give a greater insight into how the playwork perspective leads to a particular kind of adult–child relationship and practice. We believe that the tenets of this may have relevance not only across the spectrum of the children's workforce but also for parents and carers.

The approaches of other practices also have relevance for playwork which hitherto have not always been formally recognized. Guilbaud (2015:3) suggests 'Playworkers find meanings and validation for their way of being by borrowing and employing diverse perspectives' without necessarily acknowledging these shared perspectives. Jarvis, Brock and Brown (2019) explored this potential sharing of ideas about the value of play from three different standpoints – play for developing well-being; play for learning and play as an evolutionary imperative – and concluded that they were all communicating similar values and aiming for similar results – those being the well-being of children and the serving of their needs rather than those of adults. It is the interpretation of exactly what 'needs' play fulfils that is often the point of divergence. Playworkers have, at times, done as Henricks (2006:190–1) suggests when talking about Huizinga's ideas about play, 'stolen time and stood together against the world creating 'a little world of its own'; 'a special zone'.' This has not always helped playwork's status in the world nor the unique aspects of playworkers' philosophy about play itself, which underpins all their work.

'The crucial task for (us) playworkers is to engage in productive inter-professional dialogue, which recognizes and respects the differing professional cultures, values, and traditions without replicating (what we may consider to be) damaging historical professional, institutional, and gendered hierarchies' (Cullen and Johnston 2018:7) in relation to certain practices where adults hold all the power. Henricks (2009:16) defines the paradox of play being orderly and disorderly at the same time as play 'being commonly marked by shared agreements about rules, goals, environmental boundaries, team identities and the like and as a disorderly affair – in which people assert themselves against various physical social and cultural forms'. Henricks sees the importance of both, which are illustrated in the following example.

Three children at an after-school club fetched a fantasy adventure-themed board game out of the games cupboard and put it on a table. The game had a double-sided game board with a hole in the middle to represent a whirlpool, treasure cards, plastic adventurer figures and a demon king figure. The children started setting the game up with one child reading the instructions, and they called a playworker over to help them and play the game. The children and the playworker began by playing the game following the rules, rolling the die and moving their adventurer figure the required number of squares and responding to what actions the squares they landed on required. One child was very interested in their adventurer figure, picking it up and giving it 'a voice' and speaking to the other adventurer figures. One of the other children joined in picking up their figure and 'talking' to the other adventurer figures. The other child told them to stop and to put their figures back on the board and start playing the game 'properly'. The playworker encouraged them to carry on playing the game. They carried on playing the game by the rules for a few more minutes and then all three children picked up their adventurer figures and started to 'talk' to each other. They counted out '1, 2, 3' and all dropped their figures into the whirlpool hole in the board game. One child picked up the demon king figure and threw it into the whirlpool hole and then another child pushed the game board half off the table so that the figures fell through the hole and landed on the floor. The children ducked under the table, picked up the figures and ran out of the room.

In the present time and based on much historical and current research and theory, there is an important playwork approach that has much to offer. There are a set of Playwork Principles (Playwork Principles Scrutiny Group 2005) (Appendix 1) which although some playworkers may feel need revisiting is, however, a clear and simple guide to the work of playworkers. Nevertheless, the role of a playworker regularly gets conflated with, for instance childcare or youth workers and playworkers are sometimes considered to be child support workers, teaching assistants, babysitters, activity leaders and so on. Trained, qualified and experienced playworkers can find themselves understanding the importance of the playwork approach but being obliged to water it down to fit in with another professional approach. Alternatively, we have seen inexperienced playworkers and people holding different professional qualifications using an approach that, albeit would have some merit in some spheres, is not a playwork one while being called playworkers and practising something they think of as playwork. Sometimes the playwork intention is evident, but if playwork theory is not used appropriately in the practice, it may water down the value of play.

As an example of the types of compromises that playwork provision must make, Jacky describes running an out-of-school club many years ago. Despite a very cordial relationship with the school, her playwork approach was compromised due to shared use of the environment. The club had been designated a room that was also used for peripatetic music lessons, and they also had use of a playground and hall. Playwork Principle 4 (PPSG 2005) states 'for playworkers, the play process takes precedence and playworkers act as advocates for play when engaging with adult led agendas'. When children were playing in the hall or playground, Jacky had to keep them quiet as she had been asked to do so by teaching and administration staff. The 'play-room' had to be tidied and cleaned, in readiness for music lessons, while the children were still actively playing. These two things meant that the play process and the value of the playwork were diminished.

The playwork approach has a subtlety about it, which can appear simple but is, in effect, complex and difficult to communicate to others and perhaps this is why it hasn't always gained the status we believe it is due. As Grieshaber and McCardle (2010:22) say when considering 'The Trouble with Play', 'this is a call for the recognition of complexities, multiplicities, and the need for flexibility, depth of understanding and a willingness to research and to reflect on our practices, not to rely on slogans and mantras to account for what we do'. Playwork in practice is complicated – thinking about play, reflecting on it and being aware of all its different contradictions and perspectives that may influence playwork practice takes time and an open mind. As Rennie (2003:30–1) says,

> The more we understand about play, the better we are able to develop playwork practice. As playwork skills grow, its level of recognition grows, and more research is done on play. A helpful developmental spiral is created which can only benefit the child.
>
> Part of this process lies in practitioners questioning the body of knowledge and beliefs that underpin their own practice and the practice of others. Playworkers work with a change process.

Playwork lacks professional recognition in some quarters, despite having national and degree-level qualifications and a large body of information that are integral components of all its training and education, considered to be vital in relation to children's well-being. This lack of recognition means it is sometimes difficult to persuade others of the importance of allowing for the playwork approach.

We (Kilvington and Wood 2018) ask what playworkers can realistically do in the settings in which they work, if they do not have the same ethos as we have, and the managers hold different expectations that are expected to be followed by playworkers? We must acknowledge where they are coming from and its importance to them and then have personal, experiential and theoretical knowledge and understanding to support our arguments related to the importance of the playwork approach. To do this, we need to involve ourselves in reflexive reflection.

Bolton (2010: xix cited in Kilvington and Wood 2018:17) encourages us to be reflexive, to find a way to stand outside ourselves to 'examine how seemingly unwittingly we are involved in creating social or professional structures counter to our espoused values', 'being able to stay with personal uncertainty, critically informed curiosity, and flexibility to find ways of changing deeply held beliefs'.

The practice of playwork is based on both experience and theory. However, we should think about why we choose to believe that some theories are the 'right ones'. Which theories support what we believe to be the approach that should be taken by adults when supporting children's play? Why do we consider these to be the ones to follow and why not others? What is our belief related to the role of an adult when with children? Do we reject some practices without any proper basis?

We must acknowledge that playwork foremost comes from a 'play focused and child-centred perspective' and by this we do not mean that playworkers consider that they know what each child's perspective will be. Indeed, as previously said, they enter the play space or sphere of play in an unknowing way about the child's particular needs of that moment, but in a knowing way about play, its power, play types, playfulness, play environments, play resources, what sort of adult behaviour may spoil a play moment and so on.

This knowing, then, enables them to learn about the child or children at play without any preconceptions about what will happen or what the child or children's experience will be. However, that does not mean that playworkers do not understand that there are 'opportunities for taking both the child's and the adult's views of play into account' (Kane 2018:109). It is just that many adults' views of play think of it as something 'instrumental' that is useful for something else, whereas playworkers focus on it being 'an interlude' (Henricks 2006:13), with a relative absence of material consequences or a form of behaviour that can only be identified by the players as to whether it is play or not. It is purely the business of the child and 'needs no set of ulterior consequences' (ibid.).

Playworkers study much about play, including those things that are perceived as the most important aspects of play by other professionals and parents and carers. They do agree with the many potential benefits for people, adults and children that play is purported to provide, but they do not presume to know exactly what these benefits will be or have been related to any moment of play. They can only surmise but also feel confident that the play was a necessary part of the child or children's life in that moment that the playing took place, even if that was in a form and at an inappropriate time in the eyes of others. What playworkers can and should do is to reflect on what they themselves have learnt about their own involvement in a play episode; whether they consider it to have been positive and supportive or negative and spoiling or interfering; what methods of intervention were used; whether the play environment and resources offered a playful atmosphere that supported a wide variety of types of play; what types of play the children engaged in; were there any children whose play needs were not catered for; how was the play space used and so on. There are many ways that these reflections can be undertaken, and we demonstrate some of these throughout this book.

It should be stated that as in good science, the very nature of playworking is that everything is reflected upon and questioned, and this means that different ideas about play can come to the fore in different playwork times. This can lead to what Cullen and Johnston (2018:3) state in relation to the lack of professional status of playwork: 'Play is thus at risk of being subordinated to formal learning and adult-led activity and restricted to happening after children have finished their work.' Put simply, playwork is not considered as important as formal education and activity because the changeable nature of play changes the way that playwork is practised, which makes it less easy to define in a precise way.

This is unfortunate, as playwork sees ambiguity, as not being without purpose but as being appropriate to the reflective nature of playwork which, by its focus on play, is ambiguous. However, it is important for this to be rectified because although for many adult professionals, work is considered important and play is not, all playworkers share the belief that play is just as, if not more, important than work. They do accept that in the words of Delorme (2018:181), 'cultural variations and evolutionary changes in society will always provide new meanings for the role of playworkers' and 'playing (in playwork settings) will always (thus) be a flexible engagement of actions by children and playworkers based on children's (play) needs' at that time and in that place and with society as it is then.

Play, in literature, has been examined from many angles by those involved in playwork, and with an interest in play, for example, Huizinga (1955), Crowe (1983), Ellis (1973), Garvey (1977), Sutton-Smith (1997), Smith (2010), Hughes (2012), Brown (2008), Else (2009/2014), Henricks (2006), Sturrock (2007), Kilvington and Wood (2010, 2018), Lester (2020), Lester and Russell (2008), Grieshaber and McCardle (2010), Brown (2009), Singer, Golinkoff and Hirsh-Pasek (2006), Axline (1947), Newstead (2018), Spencer (1904), Hughes (2012), Callios ([1961] 2001), Bruce (2011b), Horton and Kraftl (2018).

There has always been a concern in the playwork world that it may not be possible to fully capture the experience of play and playworking by writing about it and analysing it in words. In rather the same way that a painting or a piece of music cannot be easily captured with a verbal description and analysis. Music and paintings have to be experienced to fully appreciate them. One can get so far with words, but certain things are experienced in those parts of the brain that are beyond words. This conundrum is nicely considered by Guilbaud (2015:5-6) when she suggests that 'writing about play and playworking in some way takes away from that which, when actually experienced as opposed to theorized about, play has actually been and what the playworker has actually experienced'. She suggests that it is 'playing with unknowingness' and an 'experience of negative capability'. This requires the practitioner to be able to suspend their judgements, sit with doubts, question assumptions, not be the expert adult and to resist jumping to conclusions about what has been experienced. Playworkers ask themselves lots of questions.

It is with this in mind that we set out here the widely recognized ideas and concepts about play and playwork that best support the unique approach of playwork. These include those developed within the playwork world as well as ideas based on theories from a wider field that have been developed within the playwork world. We hope they will help readers to better understand the playwork approach so succinctly described by Brown, Long and Wragg (2018) at the beginning of this chapter.

Play as an outcome

We acknowledge that play supports the intellectual, physical, social, creative and emotional development of children. In playwork, we do not plan towards any outcomes related to this. We trust that whatever and however a child chooses to play is instinctively providing whatever that child needs at that time and for their future. If we think of play as 'irrational' or as Sutton-Smith (2003) suggests as 'adaptive variability' helping children to be flexible by the processes of sloppiness, quirkiness, un-productability and massive redundancy, then we can see that play is important for its own sake. In their article about play as an outcome, Ludicology (2019:1) make a good case for focusing on play as an outcome in its own right. They suggest that if we think about play as an approach to action and as an evolutionary process 'by which children experience their lives and how they express themselves and their agency in whatever context they may be' then their opportunities for play will 'affect how they feel about themselves, the places where they live and the people they live with'. They also suggest that rather than having to measure outcomes, 'we should concern ourselves as to whether children are playing enough'. Play is a generalized approach. The value of play lies in the moments of playing.

A playworker reminiscing about her own childhood remembered one occasion as a child when her older brother helped her to fit into a suitcase. He zipped it up, carried it to the stairs and slid her down to the bottom. Her parents were not amused, but she and her brother remember with great fondness the wonderful feeling of subversiveness, risk, fun and daring they felt about this play episode.

Play as intrinsically motivated behaviour

Despite the ambiguity of play, it was necessary for playwork to come up with a workable definition that would enable it to practise in a philosophically and ethically supported manner and according to the Playwork Principles (PPSG 2005). 'Play is a process that is freely chosen, personally directed and intrinsically motivated. That is, children and young people determine and control the content and intent of their play, by following their own instincts, ideas and interests, in their own way and for their own reasons'. While this definition is still a work in progress (as suggested earlier, everything in playwork is questioned and reflected upon), the definition sets the scene for the unique nature of playwork practice – that is, in believing that behaviour cannot be classed as play unless the desire to play comes from within the child and that the child plays in whatever way he or she wishes to play, regardless of context or adult agenda. It could be said that some other professionals may feel that they see play in the same way, but they will still have their own adult agenda and will provide an environment, ambience and resources for play that are intended to support the child in achieving specific outcomes.

As a child around the age of eleven, Jacky remembers that she and her best friend used to love writing stories, that they would share with each other, giggle and moon over and never show anybody else. These were very romanticised stories and, as of the era, mainly consisted of wonderful girls at boarding schools who were much admired by younger girls; girls who owned their own horses and adventures about kidnapping, theft and intrigue. Jacky and her friend spent hours engaged in this story writing and sharing. This was play. When it came to having to write 'stories' as essays for her English class, her mind would empty. This was work that had not been internally motivated.

Play and playwork value

Play's non-literal, emotional, emergent and irrational characteristics are the basis of its value rather than its usefulness in terms of acquisition of skills (Lester and Russell 2013). The value of play lies in its ability to make life feel better; to enhance dull moments; to take us away from our 'real' lives; to unlock part of our brain that might otherwise remain locked up; to think in new ways; to experience sensations and emotions that emerge when we play. We should thus not only make sure that there is always plenty of time, space and freedom for play in children's lives, but also, we should not let moments pass when play can erupt within the everyday. On occasions, we should create magical, alternative, transformative possibilities for play to alter life.

There is more play value in some resources than in others. Newstead (2004:28) simply termed this 'the cardboard box theory', which is that 'a child can get more play out of a cardboard box than they can from whatever's inside'. Playworkers believe that 'loose parts' (materials that can be moved, carried, combined, put together, taken apart and redesigned in multiple ways) which children of any age can 'manipulate, explore, create with, change, build up and discover new uses for' (Kilvington and Wood 2018:97) – provide the best play value. Places with a wide variety of affordances (properties of the environment that offer opportunities for play) support these ideas and the notion of 'playspacetime'. In his Playwork Curriculum, Hughes (2001:23) suggests what these loose parts and affordances might consist of in a play environment supported by playworkers. In line with the playwork philosophy of concentrating on play, this curriculum focuses on the development of play types (Appendix 2) (different observable play behaviours that have been put into categories) and play possibility rather than on the development of children. (Figure 1.1.)

Figure 1.1 Chasing robots. 2017. Courtesy of Law.

Playwork's value lies in the intrinsic value of play for play's sake. However, for playwork to have this value, there must be an understanding of the theories that support it and how to practise and adapt it to the physical and social setting in which it is happening.

Jacky was gazing at the window of a big furniture shop when a large cardboard box travelling at speed rushed out of a door on the left-hand side of the shop, behind all the furniture on display and right to the other side of the shop, followed by a laughing boy of about ten years old. The box and boy disappeared through a doorway. Jacky went into the shop and made an enquiry about a screen. There had obviously been a big delivery of furniture as there were a lot of large boxes, wrappings, etc., just outside the shop door. As Jacky was leaving, one of the boxes with a bundle of heavy-duty plastic on top started wobbling and as she went by, the boy popped out from the top like a Jack-in-a-box, laughed, wobbled over, scrambled out and ran back into the shop. There's a lot of fun to be had with cardboard boxes!

Risk in play

Playwork Principle 8 (PPSG 2005) urges playworkers to balance risk with benefits for children when thinking about the play spaces and the provision of play resources they are involved with. Early years educationalists, sociologists, psychologists and others see the importance of risk-taking. Indeed, all living beings are genetically programmed to take risks to be able to develop a form of independent life. Risk-taking and the benefits of this are discussed further in Chapter 6.

Challenging themselves, overcoming fear and learning through successes and failures help children to feel independent, competent, strong and able to deal with uncertainty. However, playworkers can support children in their risk-taking by providing a place where they feel a sense of belonging and security and where non-judgemental support is available if required.

Recognizing that life holds many risks, Zinn (2016) tells us of different strategies for dealing with risk, and he talks of strategies that use a combination of expert knowledge, faith and hope, such as trust, intuition and emotion which build on experience and tacit knowledge. It is these latter which point to play as the perfect place for experiencing what it feels like to take different types of risk. To experience the results of this and build up a store of knowledge that will enable more risk-taking to happen and the benefits that this may bring. In the world of sport and business, taking risks can also lead to winning and being a success. This is discussed further in Chapter 6.

Young children of all ages play in a street in a small Andalucian white village. Their current main form of playing is on wheeled forms of transport – bicycles, carts, skateboards, tricycles, trollies, even sometimes office chairs. They whizz down the steep single-lane road that runs directly in front of houses, narrowly avoiding the local occupants who often sit or stand on their doorsteps chattering to neighbours and local dogs and young people who hang out, the latter playing football. Cars, vans, tractors and motorbikes also come down this road and so the local council put a traffic calming hump in to try and keep the speed of traffic down. This has added greatly to the fun children on wheels have in their dangerous ride down the road, as they can now fly off the hump as well as swerve to avoid other users.

Playworkers as reflexive reflectors

Reflexivity and reflection are not the sole preserves of playwork. Many other professionals such as psychologists, early years educators, therapists, teachers and learners, faith leaders and others are urged to be reflexive and practise reflection (Chinn 2007). When we talk about reflexive reflecting in playwork, we mean that playworkers are expected to look both inwardly, at themselves, their influences and behaviours and outwardly at the play environment, the playing of the children, other happenings, and their part in the whole assemblage, and to use this when assessing what happens in a playwork setting before, during and after children come to it and play. This involves them being self-aware and questioning their own attitudes, motives, behaviours, theoretical knowledge and understanding of how to use it, and to reflect on this to better recognize how these things influence the way they practice playwork. This will help them change their own behaviour if necessary but also to see how their involvement, in turn, has influence on the play environment and on the children's playing. They will then be able to work out how they can improve their practice to support the children to have richer play experiences.

When I have been working as a playworker, frequently other adults, often parents and other professionals, have suggested that being a playworker was an easy job. 'You just play with children' they have said 'How hard can that be?' as they looked round the setting seeing the children playing . . . as if that just happens by magic. What is difficult to explain is all the things we do behind the scenes to create the right conditions for things to just happen. How after each session the playworkers share their thoughts about the day, any magic moments or things that bothered them or didn't quite work out or things that need to be changed and how these thoughts and ideas influence what happens next in the play setting. How we arrive early and think about what needs doing, what resources to perhaps put out and why. How we have a continuous inner monologue going on where we are reflecting on what we are doing, or not doing and why and constantly questioning ourselves . . . what if I did this, what if I did that, should I have done that, what would have happened if I had done it differently, how will I do things differently next time, how did this impact on the children's play? As playworkers, we are entangled with lots of different aspects; physical things such as people, the children, young people, staff team, parents/carers and other professionals; things such as the building, the outdoor space, equipment and resources and emotional aspects, the moods that are generated, the flow of movement and feel of the space and different opinions, expectations, ideas and thoughts.

And while I have been trying to explain what we really do as playworkers, I have been looking over their shoulders, keeping a subtle eye on the children that are playing football who seem to be having a disagreement and assessing if I might need to intervene to cool down the tempers or if that will make it worse or if it will just sort itself out, then scanning across the playground noticing the children building a den, the children playing a game of tag and other children sitting with another playworker chatting. All the while, continuously reflecting . . .

State of unknowingness/Negative capability

As adults in the context of working with children, we have the inclination to believe that what we have been taught or what we know through our own experience – our own version of things, is the real one; the right one, the important one and one that children cannot know without our input, as they are immature and have not had the experience, education or insights that we have had. Jacky (officially now an 'old lady') says that one of the many things old age has taught her is that the things you think you know are not everybody's truth, they are an individual's interpretation of what we call facts. Our knowledge, and understanding, is very personal. 'We do not see things as they are; we see things as we are' (Attributed to Anais Nin 1961). Children know things in their own unique individual way, just as adults do, and their interpretations are just as valid as those of adults. In playwork, in the context of children playing, we never assume we are right. In fact, we assume they are right, as they are the players in their own play world. We do not impose our agendas on to them but let them create their own. To this end, Brown, Long and Wragg (2018) say it is important for playworkers to approach their role:

1. with negative capability, approaching children in a completely unprejudiced, non-judgemental and open-minded way
2. with positive regard
3. giving positive feedback (not praise as there are no right or wrong, good or bad, successful or unsuccessful outcomes in play from the adult perspective).

This unprejudiced, non-judgemental and open-minded approach, together with being in a state of negative capability, or what can be thought of as a state of unknowingness, helps playworkers to have a unique relationship with children as it puts them all on the same footing in terms of power and expertise.

Children, particularly at play, are very able to move between the real and non-real, the rational and irrational aspects of their world in a way that many adults have difficulty with. This enables them to have a knowledge that adults are unable to know unless they enter the child's world and notice in a diffuse way that they themselves are being altered by the child's play. For this to happen, the adult must momentarily be prepared to give up their adult inhibitions about what is right or wrong and true or false, and expectations as to what will or should happen, and wait for what unfolds under the auspices of the child or children's own power. It is only then that the true power of play becomes apparent.

It is important to accept that there can be some difficulty in being an adult and not using what you know or think you know while playing with a child. It takes ongoing reflection to avoid using adult knowledge and therefore potentially adulterating a game.

Jacky was playing with a four-year-old, rolling old dinky cars down two cardboard tubes; firstly, to see how fast they would travel and then how far they would go and then which went the furthest. In a moment of total involvement and fun, Jacky forgot herself and using a very old plastic car with a monkey in it, enacted a Gold, Silver and Bronze medal ceremony. The four-year-old watched, then in a very authoritative manner said, 'Right we must organize the cars and decide who is going to be the winner'. She proceeded to line all the cars up in a random fashion and roll them down the tubes one at a time and as each one stopped, she moved it into another line and from this line, chose three cars to roll down again and then declared the winner. None of this Gold, Silver and Bronze nonsense!! The game was not spoilt because of the strength of purpose of the girl.

Adulteration

In playwork, we use the term 'adulteration' for when an adult intervenes in a way that spoils the intrinsic moment and meaning of a child or children at play. Adults are often unaware that they are doing this because they have learnt to react in certain ways to certain behaviours often because of their own experience or upbringing or because of a circumstance that they encounter that they do not understand. This adulteration can occur over a variety of things such as concern over physical safety; desire to make a child happy; irritation with certain types of behaviour; desire to pass on knowledge and skills; needing to be in charge and having the power over events and more. Examples related to some of these can be found in other chapters. Reflexive reflection and team support are required to help individuals recognize their own adulterative behaviour – when and where they are spoiling children's play and then practising intervention techniques that enable them to engage with children in the play environment with as little interference in the flow of play as possible. The story where Jacky interferes with the car rolling game is a good example of adulteration.

The playwork approach

To get the crux of using the playwork approach, Kilvington and Wood (2018:42) suggest that we need to be able to do (or at least believe in the importance of doing) the following:

- Understand and utilize the philosophy behind the Playwork Principles (even if we do not wholeheartedly agree with the way that they are expressed).
- Understand the varying theories about play but, when with playing children, concentrate only on those that are about the here and now.
- Believe that children and young people do not need to be improved or developed towards adult-chosen outcomes (when playing).
- Believe that playing children intuitively play in the way that is necessary for themselves – they know better than we do.
- Try not to see everything through the prism of adult knowledge and understanding.
- Intervene as little as possible (and if necessary, in as playful a way as possible).

And we would now add:

- Reflexively reflect, alone and with others, on the setting, our own practice and other workers' practice and the children's playing.
- Keep up to date with new thinking related to play and playwork.

2
Behaviour and Adult Expectations

> **Chapter Outline**
>
> Adult and child interactions

In this chapter we shall look from different lenses, not only at how adults respond to children's varying types of, what may or may not be perceived as, play behaviour but also at the behaviour of adults in general that will influence playing children when they are together. Henricks (2009) talks of orderly play or games (governed by external rules that are made by adults or adult societal expectations) and disorderly play (freely chosen, internally motivated and often against the social order) and Henricks suggests 'play scholars should not emphasize one aspect to the exclusion of the other' (2009:2). We believe that many adults prefer orderly play.

When children are playing, we can observe their 'overt behaviour', their physical movements, use of props, interactions with other children and things and we can hear them speaking. Covert behaviour is different and more difficult to analyse as we cannot know what a child is thinking as they play or act out scenarios in their mind. Children will be conscious of some of their behaviour when playing; for example, they may actively seek to cue another child to play by throwing something at them. However, other behaviour is more instinctive. The child who has had something thrown at them may gasp in surprise but still understand the invitation to play. It is at this point that an adult may inappropriately intervene; not recognizing the behaviour as play.

Psychologists talk about rational and irrational behaviour. To adults, much of children's disorderly playing can look irrational, and probably meaningless, for example walking backwards for no obvious reason. The trained worker will be able to recognize the type of play that the child is engaging in and not consider it a waste of time, but the type in which 'strange juxtapositions and incongruities can appear without need to rationalize and justify their existence' (Lester 2020:164). Playwork only considers behaviour that may be described as play, as being play, if it has been, or is being engaged in a voluntary way. A child may appear to be playing, for instance, a game of rounders; but if this is orderly play, where the child is obliged to play to make up a team, they may not be engaged in what we in playwork would call play – merely in rounders. If the child is engaged reluctantly but one of his friends starts calling him by the name of a famous baseball player, the game may take on a different frame and suddenly the child is playing in that character and is truly playing and fully engaged in the flow of play. He has become a baseball god!

Jacky recalls, as a teenager, playing a game of tennis with a friend. *Neither of us was particularly good at the game but we made it fun and playful by commentating on shots as we were making them as if we were famous players.*

As is suggested by *paediatric doctors Davie and Butler* (2017:1), 'It is helpful to think a little more deeply about how we think about behavioural issues, an awareness of how you, parents, the child themselves and other professionals think about behaviour'. This is from an article about children with perceived behavioural issues and what the causes of challenging behaviour may be, but we think it is relevant to much play behaviour. Russell (2006:7) suggests 'given what we know about play then much of children's playing might be understood as being challenging' and she goes on to list examples such as 'obscenities, toilet humour, racism, taunts, games of power and resistance against adults' and further suggests that adults in many circumstances would see these as being unacceptable behaviour. When they are deeply involved in playing, children either behave unacceptably to protest or they do not think about whether their play is acceptable within the social order; they are in the moment, outside reality and normality. *Jacky remembers a long car journey through France, when her five children ranged from nine to fourteen years old, during which they spent much time amusing themselves making up increasingly obscene and very unacceptable names for each other such as 'Pigs Fanny', 'Dogs Bollocks' and 'Cats Piss' and singing rude songs. Their father and Jacky ignored them as they understood their behaviour as play, but we believe many adults would have felt compelled to silence this.*

Playworkers understand that play is not always nice; is often risky and testing of boundaries, possibly therapeutic and that children's play cues are often misunderstood. Russell (2006) found through her research, that when workers focus on supporting the play rather than correcting the challenging behaviour, the behaviour and atmosphere settle. Playworkers try to reflect on how the children play when they are being challenging and when they are not and the circumstances surrounding each of these. Concentrating on this, moves away from 'behaviour management' to a more therapeutic focus on why children play in certain ways at certain times. It helps playworkers to reflect on whether intervention is necessary and if so what mode or type is needed. For instance, during the long journey through France, Jacky could recognize that her children were contained for long periods of time together and could become restless, bored and irritable. She accepted that their name-calling was a playful way of passing boring, travelling time and did not interfere. However, she did pay attention to the tone of the communication play to check that it was being conducted in a playful way and would have used some form of distraction should it have seemed that it was segueing into nastiness that was designed to be hurtful. In other circumstances, the siblings would have sorted themselves out. Context is important.

Grieshaber and McCardle (2010:28) tell this story about three little girls playing at Cinderella and when the teacher notices another little girl, Lulu, watching on the edge of the game but obviously excluded, she asks the three girls if they will include her. They look at each other and agree. The teacher leaves them to it and goes around the class observing other groups playing and making notes. At the end of the session when it is time for reviewing the morning, she asks the different groups to recount their activities. When it comes to the three girls and Lulu, they excitedly talk about their game of Cinderella explaining who played Cinderella, the prince, the ugly sisters and so on, but no mention was made of Lulu. When asked what part she had played, after a glance at each other, one girl explained that Lulu had been the piece of paper in front of the fire collecting the cinders and Lulu nodded agreement. This story is told as a warning to early years teachers who may consider play as natural and therefore in some way 'innocent' and a natural means of learning. They warn that the trouble with viewing play as 'children's natural way of learning is that ideas about what is natural in children are selective' (ibid:29). Playworkers do not consider children as innocents; nor see the kind of play in Lulu's story as nice and they would not need to know what had been, or could be, learnt by any of the girls while playing in this way or any other way. However, they may reflect on their own intervention;

whether it had supported or adulterated the play and how they might respond to similar circumstances in the future. No mention is made of how Lulu felt when playing the role of cinder repository. Do you think any intervention was necessary by the teacher and if yes, what would it be and why? Were the girls bullying Lulu by first excluding her and then by giving her a strange role in the game? Could Lulu have been enjoying her role?

Julia shared a story about a child at the adventure playground who was lying down for some time. Julia was concerned that he seemed to have been there for a long time so went and laid down next to him to see if he was ok. Happily (and without being asked), he told Julia he was being a wall.

We can never assume we know how children feel about their roles when they are playing. Had Julia just asked if he were alright, he possibly would have just said 'yes' or 'no', which would have been meaningless. Had she suggested he should stand up because it was cold on the ground, she would have never had any idea as to what his lying down was all about. In both cases, she would have been adulterating the boy's play.

Playworkers consider that play should be perceived as a period outside of normal societal consequences for behaviour that may not fit within the norm: 'a common feature of children's everyday lives that contains the power

Figure 2.1 I'm not obviously watching you (but I'm here). 2023. Courtesy of Wood.

to transform children's relationships with each other and their environments' (not necessarily for the better) (Lester and Russell 2013:10). Because playworkers are present when children play, they cannot absolve themselves from their adult responsibilities, so if they feel that a child is being harmed in some way, they intervene, but in as playful a way as possible. Kilvington and Wood (2018:104–5) suggest some of these in 'everyday intervention approaches'. For instance, 'I am from the Saturn Herald, and I have heard that one of the alien enemies is being tortured. Do you have any comment, Captain?' (Figure 2.1).

We believe that many adult feelings about play are due to 'ageism' which Greenberg, Schimel and Mertens (2002:27) define as 'negative attitudes or behaviours towards an individual solely based on that person's age'. Many adults think that children, as a category, are not capable of managing their own behaviour because of their age, which leads to a stereotyped understanding of ability due to their perceived developmental status. However, those people involved in working with or living with children will know that they are all individuals and as such develop their abilities at different ages, and this should be acknowledged when it comes to their independence and their ability to choose how to play.

Rather than only thinking of adults supporting children's development, we believe that children, at play, may be able to help support adults with their development, from early adulthood through to older age. In his paper on Intergenerational Learning, Loewen says, 'Human development does not stop at adulthood. Adults frequently face many of the same challenges which adolescents face, only in different contexts and form' (1996:25) and we would say some of the challenges are the same as those faced by children. For instance, who has not seen an adult with anger management issues like those of a toddler – people suffering from road rage. Anger comes from the same part of the brain as fear and is a response to stress and perceived threats. Pellegrini (2005) thinks playing children try out, practice and refine a wide range of adaptive behaviours and approaches, experimenting with both physical and emotional uncertainty and developing strategies for dealing with stress and conflict. Perhaps those people with anger issues in later life have not resolved the use of these strategies through their playing.

Reflection Shoot the Prime Minister (from a statutory playcentre)

Sean's friends arrive and sit down to join us. They have heard about the proposal to significantly reduce service staffing levels. We are bombarded with questions primarily regarding our posts and we respond honestly, confirming that my post is at risk, but my colleagues are not, and the service will continue for the time being. Sean paces up and down in exaggerated agitation, shouting both questions and demands as he does so, 'Who do I need to ring?', 'Give me the number of the Council'. His proposals become more and more extreme, 'I know, let's shoot the Prime Minister and kidnap his children!' I wryly suggest that this may be a little extreme and perhaps would not, 'earn me any brownie points on the job front', but Sean is immersed in his righteousness and is not listening (Meares 2021).

Moss (2010) in the UNESCO briefing on Early Childhood thinks there is a general feeling that childhood is the only period of development, and that adulthood is having reached full development. This denies the ability of adults to learn, change and develop. However, in her ethnographic study, Kelly-Byrne (1989:232) demonstrates the knowledge she has acquired since she had been involved with a seven-year-old girl's play life, and this includes:

- Children have their own agendas and modes of operating.
- They are eager to share these with adults.
- They are capable of teaching adults their systems if the adults are open to seeing things from a child's point of view.
- Children initiate, plan, direct, perform and evaluate their own activities.
- They make distinction between various levels of reality.
- As such, they are highly competent meta-communicators about creating, managing and interpreting contexts for an array of their own behaviours.

Perhaps developing an understanding of the capabilities that children demonstrate when playing would be useful for all of us adults who are in some way, involved with children for the purposes of enhancing our communications and understanding of each other's behaviours.

Gilmore (2014:1) in her blog suggests that there are six life lessons that kids can teach adults – and we think play features all of these.

- To enjoy life, she thinks that even when they are going through tough times most kids can have moments of happiness, joy and freedom.
- To live in the now – 'they live with their minds, attention and energy focused on what is currently happening' – a great life skill
- To love unconditionally and forgive wrongs – despite bad experiences – kids generally can love unconditionally and forgive the wrongs of others.

- To be questioning – kids are curious, they ask lots of questions, which supports their personal growth, wellness and an openness to learn, understand and show compassion.
- To be open-minded – kids generally listen to different viewpoints and consider new ways of doing things.
- To be creative – kids are naturally creative. They sing, dance, tell stories, build, colour, make crafts and so forth without worrying about perfection (until grown-ups spoil their fun).

When it comes to playing, it seems that most adults have their own conceptualized ideas about what children should play, how they should play, what they should play with and what importance play holds in their lives, often based on their own upbringing. This leads them to deny children the right to be in control of their own play behaviour, as can be seen in the following adapted extract.

A trained playworker working in a preschool was standing with a parent watching her child during messy play in the mud table 'corner' of an outdoor play space. The parent doesn't like messy play. The playworker and mother talk about their over-particular and clean obsessed childhoods – 'cleanliness being next to Godliness'. The playworker explains her own son and the children in the setting love messy play.

Worker: *The Head of School told me that here they really value the child deciding for him/herself what they want to do because all of it is learning: sensory, social, creative, independent, scientific, and nature-based, all of it. And messy play is one way for kids to learn those things.*
Mother: *I still don't like her getting dirty.*
Worker: *You can stop her, and that's your right. But you could try letting her decide for herself whether she likes messy play? When I don't involve myself in the children's play, I see how amazingly they learn to decide for themselves and develop for themselves on so many levels. Not just the learning we were talking about before, but also a sense of their ability to work things out for themselves. I've learnt how to respect a child's right to play as they choose to, and now I feel very protective of that right.*

The mother recognizes that her child looks happy and agrees with the playworker.

Would you be able to convince a parent or carer of the value of play for play's sake?

We, (Kilvington and Wood 2018) and sociologist Lawler (2014), believe most ideas about the period that constitutes childhood are socially constructed. This means that different nations and different groups within those nations have different ideas about appropriate behaviour for children of different ages. For example, in England, the Family and Parenting Institute (2007:27) suggests that 'The law offers special protection and provision to children under 18. But the law is inconsistent'. They indicate that children of sixteen can marry, with their parents' permission and at seventeen they can take their driving test and drive a car. They are legally obliged to go to school until they are sixteen but can be taken into care until they are seventeen, and children of ten can be held criminally responsible for their own behaviour. However, they are not able to vote and are not considered to be adult until they are eighteen.

There is general agreement about certain aspects of biological development, for instance – children are physically and physiologically immature compared to adults and so there is a feeling that children need protection. In 1989, 140 countries signed up to the United Nations Convention on the Rights of the Child (UNCRC) (UNICEF 1990) but expectations regarding children's knowledge and capability vary in different cultures and at different periods in history. Children are given different responsibilities and are held legally responsible for different things, at different ages according to adult opinion. Mayall (2008:109) says that 'childhood is structured by adults' views of how their lives should be lived'. In some cultures, children have worked away from home from a very early age; some young girls are still forced into marriage; some young teenage boys become soldiers and, in many parts of the world, young people are carers in the home for younger siblings or parents and some cook and do housework from as young as seven. Some adults deny children having the capability to organize their own playing or put so many restrictions and expectations on it that disallows children to play in their own way and under their own control.

As was alluded to in Chapter 1, in most formal or informal situations where adults and children are together, the adult is the person who is in charge. This imbues the adult with a status and power – parent, teacher, scout leader and so on. These 'labels' give the adults the responsibility of 'teaching' the children appropriate ways to behave, according to different circumstances and attendant to this, the expectation that the children will behave in what is socially considered the correct way when they are perceived to be old enough to understand. Adults are expected to take steps to modify the behaviour of a child in their care if the behaviour does not fit within the parameters of that which is considered acceptable. The adult must make the decisions and is held responsible if other adults dislike the way a child is behaving.

Jacky remembers a story about one of her nephews, when he was about seven years old, and very desperate for a certain toy he saw in the shop he was in with his mother. He was making a bit of a scene, pulling at her coat and whining, and she was getting embarrassed at his behaviour. She turned to remonstrate with him, and he took advantage and cowered and said, 'don't hit me!' (even though she never did or would). She said she felt very small, as instead of other customers expecting her to curb his behaviour, she felt they would now see her as an unfit mother. After feeling humiliated and exiting the shop quickly, before she had a chance to say anything to her son, he said, 'Only playing mum!' Playing with power! Children will play anywhere.

Playworkers believe that wherever children are in a 'play setting', even a temporary one, for example, a church hall used for a children's playscheme, children should, as far as possible, be left to be responsible for their own behaviour, which may not always be approved of by adults. For example, in playgrounds with fixed equipment, there are usually no specific rules of behaviour. Children, who are not being supervised, may not just use the slide in the expected way. They may slide in many ways alone or in combination with others; they may climb up in different ways, including climbing up the slide itself, or stand or sit at the top of the slide, thus preventing other children from sliding down and so on. All this is normal play behaviour, and perhaps you will remember playing in this way. If a parent or supervising adult is present and taking notice, they will almost certainly, put a stop to much of this behaviour. Why is this? Do they think there is a 'correct' way to play on a slide? Do they think this behaviour is dangerous? Do they think that children should always share and take turns? Are they concerned about what other parents or carers will think? All the behaviours mentioned are perfectly normal play behaviour, but the reaction of adults might lead us to believe that there is acceptable 'good play behaviour' and unacceptable 'bad play behaviour'. What are your views on this and where do they come from?

Because playing is often children's default position, play behaviour does not just occur in places and at times that are designed or expected for play. It may occur anywhere.

Jacky surreptitiously observed a girl of about eleven years old cartwheeling down the long empty aisle of a large supermarket. The girl had seized the moment to play when she must have perceived no adult was watching and the long empty space cued her. She had an air of joy about her, and Jacky marvelled at the girl's ability to snatch the moment for her carefree playing. An adult, who was possibly her mother, rounded the corner into the aisle, at which point the girl abruptly halted her cartwheeling and peered into a freezer as if she was choosing something. She clearly felt that cartwheeling was not appropriate behaviour in a supermarket, although there was no prohibition notice related to children's behaviour and certainly no rules displayed that stated 'No Cartwheeling in the Aisles'.

There is a plethora of information available, for example, for parents and foster parents (National Fostering Group 2018), childcare workers (Teachwire 2023), girl guide leaders (Girlguiding 2015), social workers (Centre for Mental Health 2014) and so on, about behavioural management strategies and for education (Department for Education 2013) recommended advice on behaviour and discipline in schools. These advise how to foster what is considered 'desirable' behaviour and how to eliminate or control what is considered 'undesirable' behaviour in the 'child's best interests'. Even the UNCRC uses the term 'best interests of the child', but as Kruk (2015:1) says 'as with most articles of the Convention, however, a clear and precise understanding of the "best interest" concept remains elusive, to the point that it is subject to competing interpretations'. Even though children are sometimes consulted in matters of their welfare, it is still adults who make the decisions in most circumstances. We are not suggesting that this is wrong, but in playwork settings, children are considered experts in their own play and therefore they are left to make their own decisions about what is in their own best interests in relation to play. Generally, they are responsible for their own behaviour. Playworkers are not there to interfere in this play and must concentrate on managing their own adult behaviour so as not to adulterate or spoil the play of the child or children (even when play is not as nice as other adults might hope for), if it is not causing harm.

It is for this reason that playwork intervention has its own rules and regulations (Kilvington and Wood 2010: 88–93) about not getting involved unless children invite them to or there is a health and safety or child protection issue. Playwork Principle 8 (PPSG 2005) exhorts playworkers to 'choose an intervention style that enables children and young people to extend their play. All playworker intervention must balance risks and benefits'. In just the same way all professionals who work with children must intervene as is appropriate to the circumstances in which they are working with children, the expected benefits and the outcomes that are pertinent to their own professions. This is not to say that there may not be some crossover, but difficulties arise when adult expectations do not match the circumstances of certain types of behaviour of a child or children. An example of this occurred during a school playtime.

> *A school had been equipped with a Scrapstore PlayPod that was regularly refilled with loose parts for the children to use as they wanted during their playtimes. The playground supervisors had been playwork trained appropriate to their role. That month the pods contained several old computer keyboards, which were available to be played with in any way that the children wished to play with them. Some of them were used for role playing at offices and other types of imaginative play; some were being inspected and taken apart for object play but a couple of children were trying to smash up the ones they were playing with. The head teacher walked into the playground and spying what these children were doing shouted 'What have you done?' in an angry voice. The children stopped immediately and stood looking worried. The playground supervisors had been supervising and seeing nothing wrong had done nothing to stop this destructive playing. The playworker in charge tried to have a conversation with the head teacher explaining that the keyboards had been donated as scrap and therefore had no worth other than for being played with. She tried to explain that this type of playing was legitimate and was not related to real life. However, the headteacher would not accept that the keyboards were scrap, and the playing was just playing. She saw the smashing up as being an act of violence and stated, 'we don't have violence in school'. She was not prepared to debate the issue.*

This was playtime – not school time – and as such, the destructive behaviour was acknowledged as exploratory and object play. In the eyes of playworkers, most, but not all, children are usually sophisticated enough from a young age to be perfectly capable of understanding that different behaviour is acceptable in different circumstances. Because they were enjoying being able to try and destroy the keyboards as part of playing with loose parts, this did not mean that they would assume that it was acceptable to behave in the same way with keyboards in any other circumstances. Young people (as with adults) can be creative and destructive, and it is during playing that they can play at this in a non-real way without harming anyone and without any real-life consequences. Marsh et al. (2016:250-9) added to Hughes's (2002a) list of sixteen play types with what they termed 'transgressive play', 'Play in which children contest, resist and/or transgress expected norms, rules, and perceived restrictions in both digital and non-digital contexts' and we could term smashing up computer keyboards as transgressive play. Lester and Russell (2013: 78) suggest play 'erupts whenever conditions allow'. These conditions are 'a complex assemblage of material, symbolic, temporal, social, political and cultural factors', and conditions in a play context are provided so that 'playfulness may thrive' (ibid:212). In the playground where there were Playpods, conditions included the loose parts; the permission to play with these in any way; the understanding of the playground supervisors; the playtime release of energy; the mood and inclination of the two boys and so on.

Despite many adult concerns about children's use of technology (more fully discussed in Chapter 6) and the restrictions that they may put upon it, Marsh et al. (2016) explain that 'contemporary children use technology in different ways to children growing up in previous decades' (2016:243). They conclude that children's use of technology for play is not a diminished form of play, but sits alongside all other forms of play, and with some adaptations Hughes's (2002a) Taxonomy of Play Types (Appendix 2) can be applied in digital contexts.

Knowing how and when to intervene or not in children's playing is an important part of the role of a playworker. People who work in different spheres will have different codes of conduct or expectations for children and young people's behaviour, even if it is thought of as 'playtime'. Many adults don't think about whether they are enhancing or spoiling children's playing but more about whether the children who are playing are: developing the right sort of skills; socializing well; learning to take turns; keeping out of the way; causing too much mess; making too much noise; being unkind to somebody; likely to damage something; not using toys, games or tools in the way that they should be used; playing too dangerously; and so on.

Some adults are naturally playful, but behaving in a playful way with children can lead to the adult taking over, which may spoil the opportunity for the child to be responsible for the playing. Of course, sometimes it is fine for an adult to be in charge and/or direct activities in a certain way, but it is equally important for children to have times where they play under their own or another child's direction. It is during this type of playing that the power of play, for its own sake, kicks in. Is it acceptable for playworkers to be 'strict' and for teachers to be 'permissive'? Do you think it depends on the adult/child relationship?

Playworkers are not figures of authority; their relationship with children is immediately different from the sorts of relationships there are between most other adults and children, where there is an obvious power differential and expectations of certain types of behaviour. Mayeza (2015) gives an amusing example of this. He was carrying out research on gendered play in school playgrounds in a township in South Africa, and to obtain accurate information from the children, he spent a long time dispelling the notion that he was in an adult role when in the playground. He was eventually accepted by the children as one of them. However, he also had to obtain information from the school staff and so would help the teachers if asked. This resulted in an occasion when one of the teachers left him to be in charge while reading to the children so that she could attend a staff meeting. In his own words, 'I couldn't control the amount of chaos that erupted the minute Ms Nbada left the classroom' (ibid:59). He was not perceived to be a person with power and authority, as he had cultivated a friendly, playful relationship with the children, and therefore they did not expect him to be in control of their behaviour. Children did not show respect to Mayeza; he was not a playworker and he did not have an official role within the classroom. He had become like one of the children. However, there is reciprocity between playworkers and children in relation to respect, and if deemed necessary, playworkers can and will take control.

Account of 'an incident'

Emily, aged four (a girl who often flouted nursery rules), walked around the perimeter of her nursery playground. She held her right arm outstretched behind her while holding Suri's nose between her index finger and thumb. Emily is chatting and looking back at Suri and smiling. Suri is silent. It is difficult to make out her facial features, but she is not showing any signs of being distressed. A nursery practitioner sees this and goes over to Emily and Suri and tells Emily to stop pulling Suri around by her nose. Emily is told to go and play away from Suri and to leave her alone. The practitioner checks that Suri is alright and she appears to be fine.

The nursery practitioner rang Emily's parent to tell her that she had been involved in an incident and could she call in for a 'little chat'; something that happened quite frequently. When the parent arrived, it was explained that Emily had been seen leading a child, with limited English because she had only recently arrived in the UK, around the playground by her nose. The parent asked if the child had been injured or upset. The practitioner said the child appeared unharmed but because of her lack of English it was difficult to tell if she had known what was going on and that leading a child round by the nose was unacceptable behaviour. The parent asked if the children had been asked what they were doing or what they were playing. The practitioner replied that she did not need to ask the children as it was obvious what was happening. She said that Emily was taking advantage of Suri not being able to speak English and was bullying her. The parent said that they would talk with Emily about what had happened.

On the way home, the parent asked Emily what had happened in the playground with the other child, and Emily said she had been playing elephants and had been leading Suri by her trunk 'like you do with elephants'.

What do you think about this incident? Was the practitioner's view influenced by Emily's previous behaviour? She asked Emily to 'stop pulling Suri round by the nose'. Does the language we use to describe things make a difference? Is leading different from pulling? Was Emily bullying Suri? Was this a racist incident? Was it play? Does speaking limited English affect play? Was Suri passive and submitting to Emily? Was she unhappy? Was she silent because she was playing the elephant role? She was not smiling, so does this mean she was not enjoying herself? Do we know what Suri made of all this? Were her parents informed? What might they have thought? What would you have done? How would this be viewed in a playwork situation? What might a playworker have done?

If they were an experienced playworker – on seeing this happening – they would have almost certainly thought of it as play. It is always difficult to know if all children involved in playing are freely involved in choosing what is going on. It is important to reflect and think about everything surrounding what is happening and if there is nothing of imminent harm going to happen, take a moment to use reflexive reflection to help know whether to intervene and if so how. Using the IMEE approach (Intuition, Memory, Experience, Evidence) (Hughes 2002b:22) would mean asking yourself – what does my intuition tell me about what is going on? Did I ever play like this? What does my experience related to these children and others suggest is going on and is there some relevant theory that will help me? If the practitioner felt that some sort of intervention was required, using a playwork approach, she may have just moved a little closer to the action to be noticed watching. If there was some malign intent in Emily's behaviour this might have been enough to stop it. Or to support Suri, the practitioner could have walked around next to Suri even stooping down a little and gesturing for Suri to lead her by the nose or perhaps gesturing to Emily to see if she could hold Emily's nose and lead her around thereby making a little caravan of people. If this did not seem appropriate, then some other sort of distraction might have been used to change the play frame (the physical or emotional context for the child's playing), such as suddenly jumping up in front of Emily, in a funny sort of way, to make her stop in her tracks and maybe starting a game of follow my leader that other children could join in. If intervention is needed, playful intervention is used wherever possible to keep a playful atmosphere.

Ali shared a story from an adventure playground of a group of boys playing with blue polystyrene swimming noodles. They were taking turns to be the victim and were really hurting each other, obviously testing how much pain they could endure. The onlooking playworkers kept checking with the victims to ensure that they were still okay with this. They all said they were, and the game continued over several days. Some parents were not happy with this, and it was discovered that some of the other children were not wanting to come onto the playground because of this game. One of the players' ears started bleeding, and at this point, a playworker stopped the game. The boys said they were relieved it had stopped because they did not know how to stop it.

Testing thresholds of pain and endurance is something common in children's playing, as is purposefully hurting each other or themselves. We can think of several games such as 'how long can you hold your breath for?' 'Who raps whose knuckles first?' 'How long can you endure this ever-tightening wrist burn?' Sometimes children will invent make-believe games that involve an element of physically hurting each other. It may seem as if the game has been devised to try out inflicting or receiving pain. Many of us have heard the retort, 'I was only playing!'

How do we identify bullying behaviour over play behaviour? This is not always easy and is to a certain extent a judgement call based on what is happening and reflecting on previous experience of the child or children involved. Gill (2007:44) gives an example of his daughter playing with friends in a local park and running to him to say 'Dad, those boys were bullying us' when neither she nor her friends had ever met the boys before and after announcing this ran off again to play. Bullying is not everyday teasing, name-calling and so on. Real bullying is intended to hurt another person; it is repetitive; it uses emotional, psychological or physical aggression, and it involves the use of power.

There is, rightly, a lot of emphasis on dealing with bullying as it can have a devastating effect on children's lives. However, Gill (2007) suggested this may have been leading to children and adults identifying behaviour as bullying, that is actually teasing, challenging or critical comments and a part of all normal childhood interactions. This is not to underplay the distress that real bullying causes, but to suggest that to overprotect children may cause them to feel like 'victims' whenever they are upset by another child's behaviour and may prevent them from developing the skills necessary to face difficult situations in adult life with confidence. Besag (2002:192) says 'The role of adults in the playground is to be vigilant and supportive, ready to step in, but only where necessary'.

Russell (2006) trained a group of playworkers, using the playwork theories to analyse challenging and bullying behaviour in the context of playwork and to support playful responses that would contain the behaviour, thereby also protecting other children from the effects. An example of this is related to an aggressive boy who would repeatedly turn play fighting into aggressive fighting that hurt others. First, recognizing the benefits of play fighting, the playworker challenged the boy to a play fight to avert a real fight and then introduced pillow fighting, with rules and boundaries which enabled the emotions of play fighting to be experienced within a play frame and meant other children joined in as they were no longer scared of being hurt. A child who bullies needs help as much as a child who is being bullied.

Play settings have a different ambience than that of schools and other settings, and thus playworkers have a different relationship with the children. Hughes (1996:48) writes of 'ambience indicators' for play settings, such as empowering, friendly, caring, non-judgemental, alternative, respectful, safe, secure, sanctuary and unthreatening. Playworkers supervise from the perspective of trusting the children, but in certain situations observe in an analytical and diagnostic way (Hughes 2002b) where it is perceived there is or may be a problem that needs to be dealt with. In the story about Emily leading Suri 'an elephant' around by the nose, we give examples of how a playworker may have intervened to change the atmosphere of play when there may or may not have been an element of bullying.

By interacting with children as their equals and behaving naturally in a non-adulterating way, playworkers get to know children as they really are and are in a good position to recognize if a child is a potential bully or being bullied. They have the sorts of relationships with children that enable them to 'chat' about things that the children might feel uncomfortable or threatened by talking with adults who are in positions of power. Playworkers do still have the same responsibility as other adults who work with children to report concerns if they think a child is being harmed in some way, but they are always in support of children's right to play whatever the circumstances. 'We (adults) indeed all have a role to play that can benefit children, and consequently all of us' (Kilvington and Wood 2018:152) and thus it behoves us all to think about our own behaviour just as much as the way we respond to children's behaviour, no matter how difficult that may be.

3
Education

> **Chapter Outline**
>
> Children learn naturally through play

'Education, education, education'. So famously said by Tony Blair at the UK 1996 Labour Party Conference when setting out his election priorities before winning a landslide victory the following year. But he was not a voice in the wilderness – education reform has always been an ongoing political theme for many governments around the world, with many political parties using it as a weapon or a bargaining chip to gain power or curry favour. Politicians seem to have plenty to say about education and how, where and why it should take place and what it should comprise, though few of them have been teachers themselves.

But while most people agree that education is a good and necessary thing, the very word itself can mean different things to different people, depending on their philosophical standpoint and sociocultural background. And the relationship between play and learning and how this works naturally and/or could be nurtured has been a subject of debate for decades. Considering the following questions can help the reader identify his/her own position on this.

How do I/did I think and learn?
What is the purpose of education?
What is the role of the teacher?
What is the role of the student?

How should a teacher teach?
What should be taught and who should decide this?
Do we learn from/by/through playing?

Do any of the following diverse possibilities 'fit' your views – or fit your own experiences of education?

The purpose of education is to

- civilize – equip children with morals and particular knowledge so they can be effective adult members of society;
- coach – instruct children in how to perform a specific action or role and/or how to academically achieve;
- develop – encourage and foster questions and exploration of ideas;
- indoctrinate – systematically drill learners with specific beliefs or facts to be accepted without question;
- enlighten – illuminate and inform children with theories and subjects new to them;
- inspire – motivate and stimulate children to pursue particular concepts or topics;
- mentor – advise and counsel learners in ways of thinking or doing;
- nurture – encourage and cultivate children to learn and achieve;
- train – direct and discipline children in certain behaviours and information as members of the future workforce;
- socialize – enable children to develop and appropriately use social skills.

We have likely all experienced some or even all of the above at different times and will therefore prefer some to others, but it does beg the question 'How and what should we be teaching children and young people?'

For many centuries, children informally learnt from those around them the knowledge and skills they needed to survive, either through observation and practice or being shown. And of course this still happens – children have always learnt from each other, from parents and from other adults. Formal schooling of the masses, however, is quite recent historically in terms of first teaching literacy and numeracy, and then science and social sciences as a wider knowledge base began to be deemed necessary to equip the future workforce. But therein lie the questions that this chapter is attempting to address. If formal education exists to prepare the next generation to participate in society, earn a living and survive whatever events and issues arise, what should it comprise, and how should it happen? How do children best learn?

And the important question for us is, what has play got to do with any of this if, as Ackerman (1999:11) says, 'play is our brain's favourite way of learning'?!

Let us begin by looking at current trends in education. The coronavirus pandemic has had a huge impact across the world in many spheres and caused us to rethink many societal issues. Formal education in its usual mode had to suddenly change – an estimated 90 per cent of children worldwide (Human Rights Watch 2021) had their education disrupted and most children stayed at home. Schools had to teach online and/or remotely and send home set tasks so that children could continue to learn. But it quickly became clear that it was not a level-playing field and that some children were more vulnerable and disadvantaged. Access to laptops, internet connection and learning support/resources was not as available or possible for everyone. Learning online did not suit all children – although some fared better by not being in the classroom. Parents' responses in adjusting to this varied hugely – some tried to directly help with lessons and homework, some involved children more in activities like cooking, gardening, DIY and crafts, others decided to just let children play, others needed children to help with housework and/or caring for relatives, and of course, many parents did some or all of these things. But the unprecedented situation caused wider discussions and questions on social media about the purpose of schools, different kinds of both teaching and learning, what learning was essential and who should decide this, what was 'lost learning' and how children could 'catch up' and how the 'digital divide' could be overcome. Barnado's (2020) also reported and made recommendations on the role schools should be playing in supporting children's mental and emotional health. There has been increased interest in home education, outdoor learning, forest school and alternative education and how to better support learning for children with additional needs (Harvey et al. 2021, Hattenstone and Lawrie 2021, Eveleigh 2022). In all, there has been wider recognition that one size does not fit all and that going forward we need a more balanced approach and a wider curriculum that is also practical, creative and engaging.

Experiencing the educational effects of the pandemic has widened such debate, but there were already campaigns that were calling into question recent educational trends. In the last three decades, there has been an increased scolarization process in the UK and in many other countries too, through:

a) the introduction of national curricula so that all schools teach the same subject content

    b) a move to limit or restrict recess/break times to increase learning time
    c) an increase in assessment and testing
    d) an increase in class sizes
    e) a reduction in the coverage of creative and practical subjects and 'soft skills'
    f) greater financial and business management of schools.

(Baines and Blatchford 2019, Williams-Brown and Jopling 2020)

These changes were initiated by policymakers and many in the teaching professions were – and still are – deeply unhappy about them (Wood and Attfield 1996, Brock et al. 2009, Moyles 2010, Andrews 2012). Jarvis, Brock and Brown (2019:3) argue that 'Education practices have become too heavily skewed towards the narrowly traditional, driven by the neoliberal goal of producing compliant consumers and workers for the international marketplace . . . such a practice has its roots in a philosophy of "dehumanisation" (and) it should not be a surprize that the subtleties of child development begin to become invisible'.

The discontent shown by professionals seems to show up a fundamental mismatch between policymakers and professionals and sometimes between teachers themselves, regarding how children learn and what and how children should be taught. There are of course a multitude of ways in which individual children learn, but if it is possible to put something that is clearly complex into simple terms, this mismatch is perhaps about learning being adult-directed or child-directed and the possible spectrum between the two. Even these terms, however, can have multiple interpretations. Adult-directed can mean didactic instruction to passive learners, but it could also mean a teacher choosing and planning to cover a particular topic with the full intention of stimulating participation and inspiring query. Child-directed could mean that a child has full choice in what and how they learn and that they pursue only what interests them without the need for any adult involvement, but it could also mean that a child seeks adult support and information on a topic of interest (which may also have been anticipated or previously initiated by the adult). So perhaps the mismatch – and the argument – is more honestly about control – who is controlling (or trying to control) what is being taught and/or learnt and how this happens? 'Children come into the world burning to learn and genetically programmed with extraordinary capacities for learning' says Gray (2013:x) but he goes on to argue that we turn this off 'with our coercive system of schooling'. Briggs and

Hansen (2012:4) agree – 'our education system appears to have failed children for whom learning is no longer a fun activity but a tedious means to an end'. As Pellegrini says, 'children are more concerned with process than with product – but adults want them to get to the conclusion' (2009:198). He also states, 'we as researchers and teachers must come to realize that different types of children learn in different ways and that structural views of development and teaching which minimize or ignore individual differences are doomed to fall short as individuals often take different routes to competence' (ibid:212). This does rather contradict the concept of an imposed and compulsory national curriculum.

Interestingly, while Western governments have been trying to emulate teaching methods from countries in East Asia, which have been consistently topping the Programme for International Student Assessment (PISA) tables in maths, reading and science for many years, attention in Singapore, Japan, Korea and Hong Kong is now 'shifting from a uniform, teacher-centered, exam-oriented pedagogy towards diverse, student-centered learning pathways that aim to instil capabilities for lifelong learning' (Kattan and Bend 2018). While the West has been bringing in national curricula and standardized testing, East Asian countries 'have been expanding and redefining education outcomes to include what are commonly known as 21st century skills: creativity, communication, collaboration and higher-order thinking; they are also interested in students' social, emotional and physical health' (Zhao 2017) because they now recognize that exam-oriented education causes 'high anxiety, excessive stress, poor eyesight, lack of confidence, low self-esteem and lacking life skills' (ibid).

Over the same period of recent scolarization, there have been reported increases in learning 'disorders' or learning difficulties such as dyslexia, autism, attention deficit hyperactivity disorder (ADHD), pathological demand avoidance (PDA), although there is also scepticism about how genuine this rise in childhood disorders is (Robinson 2010). It is not clear whether we are getting better at recognizing and diagnosing what was already happening, whether there is 'over-diagnosis' to procure additional support, whether some 'disorders' such as 'social phobia' are actually the labelling of everyday emotions (Guldberg 2009:21) or whether there is a real increase in children's learning difficulties. There has also, however, been charted increases in stress-related mental illnesses in children and young people (Twenge 2000) with Twenge reporting that depression and anxiety have considerably and consistently increased in children, adolescents and college students over the decades since the tests were first developed in the early 1950s. Like Gray (2013), we do wonder if play deprivation could be a contributing factor here, especially when the very '21st century' skills listed earlier that are most needed in our young today are a natural outcome of self-directed playing.

Theorists and educators of young children have long promoted the importance of play in learning (Piaget 1962, Plowden 1967, Bruner 1966, Vygotsky 1978, Moyles 1989) because children's natural drive to play results in so much exploration and discovery. We have written elsewhere (Kilvington and Wood 2016) regarding the many other theories about the purposes of playing, not least for brain growth and physical, emotional, social and cognitive development, which we will not reiterate here. Evidence continues to mount, however, to show that play is fundamental to and critical for human development and experience, and it therefore has a momentous role in education.

Could it be that the move away from a more playful and child-centred education to a more adult-directed curriculum is therefore a relevant factor here? Has the trend towards a 'one size fits all' curriculum with constant testing and assessment been a causal factor in children finding it harder to learn and feeling increasingly unhappy, as East Asian countries now believe? If so, there is even more of an imperative to find ways to keep children at the heart of education – and that will include recognizing the power of play and allowing it to flourish in our classrooms and school playgrounds. We agree with Sigman (2015:3) that 'policymakers should consider child's play in a very serious light' and that children should have more regular opportunities for play, including physical play, in school. We would argue that play – and the playwork approach – is equally significant to the role of educators.

'Teachers are arguably the most important group of play professionals, yet they receive a minimal amount of training in the field in comparison to others such as playworkers and play therapists' (Howard and McInnes 2010:34). In the UK in the 1990s, 'the move towards a traditional, subject-based curriculum resulted in most initial teacher training courses focusing mostly on how to deliver subject knowledge' (Brock et al. 2009:28). Looking at the Initial Teacher Training (ITT) core content framework (Twiselton et al. 2019) on the UK Department for Education's website, it does indeed show that teachers are trained to

1. set high expectations;
2. promote good progress by presenting material that can be understood and remembered;

3. demonstrate a good subject and curriculum knowledge;
4. plan and teach well-structured lessons;
5. adapt teaching to incorporate individual differences and knowledge level;
6. make accurate and productive use of assessment;
7. manage behaviour effectively;
8. fulfil wider professional responsibilities.

Where, however, is the subject content for would-be teachers about children and young people themselves – how they develop, how they communicate, how they learn and what they feel? Is there not a hidden agenda here that still regards children as needing adult input as they are unable themselves to self-regulate – rather like the 'savages' in Golding's *Lord of the Flies*? Do we see them just as future beings that need to be taught and equipped, or as human beings with a full life to live in the present? Do we believe that children have an innate humanity, and do we trust them?

And as we know that play features highly in children's physical, social and emotional development, their communication and learning, where is the input for future teachers on play itself and how to foster and support this both inside and outside of the classroom? From our research, there is some minimal coverage in modules entitled professional practice for first-year students in early years teacher training, but it takes some finding and does not stand out as core content. The UK national curriculum itself only mentions the word 'play' once and then only in the context of role-play.

In early years education where there has traditionally been a history of play-based education, several authors (Brock, Jarvis and Olusoga 2019, Andrews 2012, Grieshaber and McCardle 2010, Fisher 2016) lament that 'there is still a lack of affirmation from parents, from primary school teachers and from headteachers regarding the place of play in learning in a school environment' (Brock et al. 2009:29).

Even in the early years, there has also been a complicated history of the concepts of play and learning and how to reconcile this in everyday practice. But

> what history does tell us is that there are many ways of viewing the child and their play activity and we should adopt a broad perspective, different from thinking of play as a child's work, a vehicle for learning or merely as recreation or release. Play is both created by, and creating of, culture; it is informed by society and science; it creates health and future resilience and offers opportunities to practise responses to the unknown. It is perhaps about

spirituality and an instinctive connection to the past. It has been tested for generations. Essentially, it is a right that children have, to explore and practise a range of skills, concepts and relationships that have meaning for them, not merely something to be shaped by those adults to meet blunt education targets. (Andrews 2012:56)

How can teachers teach against a given curriculum and still promote and support play and use play as a learning tool, and additionally still share control of this process with children themselves? Let us look at some examples that we have seen or have been shared with us by teachers and teaching assistants, and then explore the logistics of this further.

A playful attitude

Having a playful attitude in the first place has several advantages. Children naturally warm to playful adults and feel they are much more on their wavelength. Playfulness often involves fun and humour, and when this is a natural part of lessons, it encourages attention and participation. Being playful also involves being flexible, which increases the opportunity to include children with different needs and learning styles. Responding playfully to children can defuse growing tension and distract them. This does not mean that teachers become clowns or entertainers; it means they recognize that play is hugely important to children and so find playful ways of responding to and communicating with them – in effect, they are giving permission to children to be their natural playful selves. The following examples were observed in a primary school.

> *Conor (aged ten) struggles with paying attention and relating to others and often behaves in a way that challenges adults in the classroom. On this occasion, he had decided to block the doorway so that no-one else could get in or out of the classroom. The teacher asked him a few times to move, but he took no notice. The pastoral care leader got called to intervene and 'deal with' Conor. She came to the door saying, 'oh a puzzle to solve – I do love a puzzle' and studied him for a few seconds, whereupon she then got on her knees and went through his splayed legs saying 'Dadaa!' Conor laughed and immediately relaxed, declaring that 'Mrs T is a nutter' and went with her to his desk, where she then asked him what work he was doing and showed interest in it.*
>
> *Katya aged eight, has occasional meltdowns or shutdowns that are difficult to come back from and needs time out to calm down. On this occasion, she had*

just 'gone inside' herself and was not speaking. Mrs K, the teaching assistant, took her into the corridor and seeing a spacehopper spilling out from a resources cupboard, spontaneously said to Katya to 'hang on while I just go and fetch myself' and proceeded to get on the spacehopper and bounce all the way down the corridor and back with a crazy expression. Katya smiled and when invited by the teaching assistant to 'fetch herself too', got on another spacehopper and the two of them went bouncing up and down the corridor and laughing. Katya went happily back into class a few minutes later.

A teacher of six to seven-year-olds was explaining what prepositions were to a class and noticed that many children looked blank. She went over to a box of toys in the corner and got a duck. 'This is Melbourne Duck children, and he knows all about prepositions. He only said to me this morning that he would like to help all of you learn about them, didn't you Melbourne?' Melbourne duly 'nodded' and then 'spoke' in the teacher's ear. 'He wants you all to say hello to him, will you do that?' All the children perked up and chorused 'Hello Melbourne Duck!'. The teacher then proceeded to use the duck to show what prepositions were, by hiding Melbourne behind a box, standing in front of a pencil case, sitting on top of the desk etc. with the teacher talking to or through the duck the whole time – illustrating playfully and perfectly what prepositions mean and how they are used . . .

These are simple but highly effective spontaneous examples of a playful attitude – communicating playfully with children to gain their cooperation, gain their attention and/or to explain a topic. Such an attitude recognizes that children do perceive the world differently from adults and so seeks to enter their world, rather than demand they enter ours. This approach cannot be easily taught as a methodology, it must be authentically experienced in the moment.

Creating playful environments

This can include both classrooms and both indoor and outdoor spaces to play during breaks. Classrooms are learning environments, but if they also contain 'playthings' that can be used as teaching aids, for exploration and discovery, or for distraction and relaxation, this not only is more appealing to children, but can maximize learning opportunities. Such playthings can include toys, puppets, board games, dressing-up clothes, and so on, but also both specific and random props (playworkers call these loose parts) like magnifying glasses, cardboard boxes, strips and pieces of different fabrics, jugs, bowls and funnels, lengths of cane, balls of string and tape, buttons – the list would be never-ending – which can be called upon at any time to illustrate a point or set a challenge or be explored. Creating a more flexible environment by increasing access to objects and props that can symbolize whatever children's imagination prompts, then also employs and maximizes the flexibility in children's brains so that they can then make new connections and pose ever new questions. Brown (2002:60) describes this ongoing cyclical process and calls it 'compound flexibility'. Knight says, 'as an adaptive species with the capacity to create unique solutions to problems, we need an environment that prompts us to the kind of "fiddling about" (play) that leads to discoveries and understandings' (2016:142). Loose parts 'engage, support and enrich all types of learners and learning intelligences. Open ended learning, experimentation, problem solving, and critical thinking are all developed through the use of loose parts. These are all important skills to develop in a rapidly changing world' (Play Wales 2020a). In a problem-filled world that is going to need a lot of novel solutions, it is ever more important that children can access such rich and flexible environments.

Similarly, school playgrounds, playing fields and halls or corridors, if children are inside, should be playful spaces that interest, stimulate and invite children to be themselves. All too often, primary schools invest in expensive climbing frames or ground markings in the belief that these will occupy children and/or encourage cooperative play, only to find that children quickly get bored with these and/or use these 'improperly'. Outdoor Play and Learning (OPAL) has been helping schools in the UK and Canada to see their outdoor spaces through children's eyes and make them more available and inviting. Similarly, the Playpods project initiated by Bristol Children's Scrapstore and delivered across the UK and in France and Spain trains those adults who supervise school playgrounds and installs 'playpods' – containers full of loose parts for children to play with at lunchtime. (Figure 3.1)

Initiatives like these involve a recognition of children's natural drive to play and cultivate a positive attitude that permits and supports messy, risky, creative and imaginative play in any weather, rather than stopping it or creating obstacles or rules that disallow it. A couple of examples we have seen are given here.

A rainy weekend meant that some parts of a school playground were muddy. Quick-thinking lunchtime supervisors grabbed a roll of pedal bin liners and some tape so that children who wanted to could create temporary 'overshoes' and still go and play and they also taped up a roll of paper on a wall. This simple

Figure 3.1 Making your own space at school matters. 2019. Courtesy of PRC.

playful permission prompted a whole raft of new imaginative games and mud painting that day, which in turn initiated staff discussions that resulted in collecting scores of old wellies (rubber boots) from parents and the building of a wooden wellie stand to store these for future playing.

A teacher acquired a dozen off-cuts of climbing rope from an adventure centre and made these available for lunchtime play in a school that had recently installed a playpod. Among other things, the children used these to make swings (by attaching these to a sturdy metal rail inside the playpod). The headteacher came out to observe play that day and watched while a dozen or so children initially tried to erect their own swing in the same small space. Rather than immediately intervening to tell them not to do this and why, she stayed close by and watched to see what would happen. Left to their own devices, children soon got themselves organised, helped each other with knot-tying to eventually make two swings, created rules for turn-taking, tried out different methods and tested out what weight each swing could carry and what lengths they should be. The headteacher said she was astonished at not only how much they discovered and talked about gravity, calibration and measurements, but how much 'children of all ages worked together and were sensible – I had no idea they were so capable!'

Ardelean, Smith and Russell (2021:4) helpfully frame their argument about the value of playtimes in school by describing their intrinsic value (children's ownership and enjoyment), their instrumental value (e.g. play's value as a springboard for learning or cooperation) and institutional value (the value of great playtimes to the wider school and stakeholders, for example, for increased classroom attention and fewer playground conflicts).

The examples given above are from schools that are on a journey of understanding that the intrinsic value of play – that is, children's genuine ownership and enjoyment of their playing – is crucial and that the other kinds of value (which tend to matter more to adults) will not be manifested without this.

It is our view that one of the reasons for the ongoing success and growth of the OPAL programme is that OPAL mentors always start with the full agreement and cooperation of the head teacher, knowing that without that they will fail. It is the head teacher who defines and sets the culture in a school, and if that culture does not include understanding of and permission for play, then any other initiatives or projects to improve playtimes and playgrounds will not succeed long term.

We recently saw a set of rules up on the wall in a school playground that, refreshingly, were not a list of don'ts (which we have seen many times), but on closer examination, these were basically asking children not to play, because that would be the actual consequence of observing rules like 'keep your hands and feet to yourself', 'only say nice things to others', 'let others join in your game', 'play sensibly' (there's an oxymoron!) and 'always go to an adult if you have a question or a problem'. How can children be free to be themselves and be with their friends if they are being told to obey such rules? How can they sort things out for themselves, negotiate with others and let off steam? Any adult who tells a child to play nicely or play sensibly has not understood play and its myriad of manifestations. Even in a great physical play environment, if the understanding of and permission for freely chosen play is not also present and communicated, then the environment may as well be a prison yard. Spaces comprise both the affective atmosphere as well as the physical landscape/resources, and the former is determined by the attitudes of the adults who are present. If children don't feel free to be themselves and play in their own ways, then it doesn't matter how wonderful the physical environment is; play will be at best minimized and at worst, crushed.

Sadly, as well as life-enhancing examples of play and playful adults in schools, we have also seen the following, and these are not isolated incidents:

- a child who had playfully bopped another child on the head with a piece of foam (which didn't hurt) being soundly told by a headteacher that this was an act of violence;

- a headteacher saw children taking it in turns to drop-kick a soft toy animal (they were having a competition) and told them this was a horrible and disturbing thing to do;
- a teacher ran out and stopped some children chasing another child because she perceived it as bullying and never stopped to listen that they were playing aliens on the planet Zob and saving the universe;
- another teacher literally bellowing at five-year-old children to listen, stand still, and, on her word, march smartly and properly into the hall as though it were a military parade.

It is deeply worrying that instances like this are happening every day in schools across the world, to control and socially educate children. But if teacher training does not include participative and explorative sessions and workshops on child development and the fundamental importance of play, perhaps it is understandable. Ali's four-year-old grandson came out of school at the end of his very first week with a sad face and said, 'Grandma can you please talk to my teacher, because she doesn't understand the difference between play-fighting and real fighting'. He knew the difference and his fellow pupils did too.

The conditions for play to thrive in school include permission, time and space (Play Wales 2020b) and play materials including loose parts. Permission seems to be the hardest won here. We have seen schools making both time and space but still battling with permission because giving over control to children to play in the ways that are meaningful for them is hard for adults who have been taught to be in control in the classroom. It is difficult to see the world through children's eyes, to see that play is their normal modus operandi and to value it as they do. 'It is difficult to let go of the idea that adults know best, or at least be seen to know best' (Appleton 2002: 51) and we must agree that 'the adult world has lost contact with what it is to be a child' (ibid:68).

Having trained adults in play and playwork for many years, it is almost always a eureka moment early on when they emotionally reconnect with their own childhood memories of playing and realize they have forgotten that children experience the world very differently from adults. Feedback after undertaking such training consistently includes comments that it has helped them be better parents, teachers, social workers, carers and so on (although that was not a planned intention). Increasing genuine play opportunities and understanding and using the playwork approach in school can pay huge dividends, and evidence shows that behaviour improves, concentration increases, children are healthier, happier and more resilient and adults are happier too! (Ardelean, Smith and Russell 2021, Baines and Blandford 2019). It is a real mind-shift, however, requiring a flattening of the normal hierarchical relationship between adults and children, a profound respect for children, and a recognition that given opportunity, children are far more capable and competent than we ever realized. Korczak still reminds us that we are mistaken if we think we have to lower ourselves to communicate with children. Instead, '. . . we have to reach up to their feelings. Reach up, stretch, stand on our tip-toes' ([1925] 1992:3).

As Howard and McInnes say, implementing play in the classroom is 'a way of practice that requires in-depth training and continuous reflection by the practitioner' (2010:31). Developing such a mindset does require commitment, observation and reflection, self-awareness and a willingness to keep an ongoing open mind – a big ask of adults who are often already stretched and stressed, but one that is worthwhile and definitely unregrettable.

Planning for play

As well as cultivating a playful attitude, promoting free play and creating playful environments, some schools have also incorporated a more playful approach in their lesson planning. Outdoor learning – taking the classroom outside is becoming more popular, as is including forest school sessions in the wider curriculum. Outdoor Classroom Day is a global movement to encourage schools and families to enable children to spend some time outdoors every day (see www.outdoorclassroomday.org.uk). Selhub and Logan (2014) talk of regular experience in the natural world providing a 'pathway of change' in terms of enjoyment in learning, greater awareness of self and the surrounding environment and increased synaptic connections. Knight (2016) shows how regular forest school sessions are relevant and effective for all ages and all abilities for their cognitive development and emotional health. Regular playful learning outside promotes 'uncertainty, agency, authenticity and mastery' (Beames and Brown 2016:6) all of which are much harder to allow and experience in an imposed curriculum and all of which are necessary for survival in today's world.

Besides offering regular open play sessions, some adventure playgrounds have begun offering school visits in the daytime. One we know well in the West Midlands began doing this initially as a means of generating income and offered playful forest school sessions and the John Muir environmental award to local schools and pupil-referral units. Over time, however, it was clear to their teachers that while children and young people were achieving these awards and gaining knowledge in ecology and wildlife, they were also experiencing increased attention and concentration, gaining skills in tool use and fire management, reporting feelings of happiness and achievement, showing greater self-awareness and improved social skills. Interestingly, young people who had been excluded from mainstream school and were attending pupil-referral units seemed to benefit the most, and one does wonder whether if plenty of regular outdoor play and learning were the norm for all children throughout their childhood, this might solve many current issues and reduce the number of school exclusions. Perhaps the obsession of children reaching specific standards at specific stages is really missing the point that children learn at different paces and have a broad spectrum of needs to be met, not just academic (Appleton 2002). Briggs and Hansen (2012:65) describe the 'planning paradox' for teachers and suggest that they recognize their roles as manager, facilitator and player, moving between these accordingly so that there are sufficient and serendipitous opportunities for child-led activities because 'we know that children learn best when they are motivated and part of that motivation comes from being in control of their learning and following areas of enquiry in which they are interested' (ibid:17).

There are a few hundred democratic schools around the world that ascribe to the ethos that children themselves should shape their own education, that lessons should be chosen and not compulsory and that children should have freedom to pursue their own interests and how they spend their time. These schools are run as democratic communities with staff and children all having an equal vote in how they operate. Perhaps the most famous of these are Summerhill in England and Sudbury Valley in Massachusetts, USA. For many people, these schools are an anathema – visitors have come away with over-dramatized horror stories of 'the school with no rules', convinced that children are allowed to regularly swear, smoke and have sex. The idea that children can be trusted to regulate their own lives and make sensible choices about what they do and how they learn causes deep cognitive dissonance for many adults because such an ethos does not fit with current social paradigms that regard children in need of our protection and education and therefore unable to make any decisions in these areas for themselves. Democratic schools, however, believe that children are 'innately wise and realistic' (Neill 1962:20) and therefore treat children as colleagues rather than pupils. There are regular community meetings attended by both children and teachers where anyone can raise issues about school life, which are then openly discussed and potential solutions voted on. Everyone has one vote and there is an understanding that everyone's views are to be heard and respected. Children are fully involved in law-making and day-to-day management and take this seriously. They decide themselves whether or not to go to classes and which classes to attend, and a great deal of their time is given over to imaginative and creative playing and finding out things for themselves. Follow-up of past students shows that the majority go on to further or higher education and/or find enjoyable employment as well as exhibit high levels of confidence and resilience. So why are there not more such schools? Is the idea of adults ceding control to children so different and difficult that it seems impossible or simply wrong?

The ethos of democratic schools is very similar to playwork in that there is a profound respect for children and an understanding that they pursue their own interests through playing. This may explain why playwork training often causes similar cognitive dissonance and why playworkers often strive to be understood when explaining their craft – because play in all its ambiguity (Sutton-Smith 2009) defies definition and control by anyone other than the player. To be so misrecognized, Fraser posited, 'Is not simply to be thought ill of, looked down upon or devalued in others' attitudes, beliefs or representations. It is rather to be denied the status of a full partner in social interaction, as a consequence of institutionalized patterns of cultural value that constitute one as comparatively unworthy of respect or esteem' (2000:113). Perhaps the same institutionalized patterns prevent recognition of the value of teachers in democratic schools too (and teachers striving to be playful in mainstream schools) and point to the need for deeper intra-professional debate.

This was well explained in a recent article by Cullen and Johnston (2018) describing a pilot project employing playworkers in primary school classrooms and the consequent debate around professional power and recognition. A 'tacit acceptance and agreement (by the school) of the importance of play' (ibid:478) does not go nearly far enough in practice, without an examination of the power relationships between adults and children – the old thorny problem of recognizing the difference between 'espoused theory' and 'theory-in-use' (Argyris and Schon 1974:23) is crucial here. In the evaluation of this pilot project, the 'negative capability' of the playworkers was noted, that is, their ability to 'accept uncertainties, mysteries, doubts, without any irritable reaching after fact and reason' (Keats 1817) meaning that in practice, they were happy not to be experts in any way and to form relationships with children without making demands. This of course caused a warm reciprocal response from children and consequent engagement in learning. But if teachers are to support play and playfulness in the classroom, they will need to understand that this cannot happen without their willingness to equally engage with uncertainty and a shift in the balance of adult–child power. As Cullen and Johnson conclude (2018: 479), 'the seemingly chaotic and anarchic qualities of play may be disconcerting and cause teachers to feel a loss of control', yet it is these very features that render play so valuable for children's development, well-being and learning. Such negative capability is not passive – 'it is not sitting back, spacing out and doing nothing. It is really being aware of the situation without jumping to conclusions and leaping to intervene' (Fisher 2008:178). Play itself is powerful and we need to trust children with it and equally, if we dare to hold our breath in that moment and in the space as play arises, also trust our own intuition to support it.

Promoting and supporting play and playful learning in schools is certainly both desirable and possible. If more schools could think of their pupils as colleagues but with different roles, then it would, at a stroke, create more harmony and understanding (Clifton 2014). We agree with Holt that 'children are smart, eager to learn, eager to play a useful part in our world' (1970:298). By cultivating a playful attitude, creating playful environments and planning for play from infants onwards, right through to the end of secondary school, teachers and teaching assistants the world over are in a unique and privileged position to support the learning of children of all ages.

UNCRC Article 28 describes children's right to full-time education, but without equal recognition of (a) their right to express their opinions and have them taken seriously (Article 12), (b) their right to freely express themselves (Article 13) and (c) their right to freely play (Article 31), adult-directed education will not equip children to be the autonomous, creative, investigative, social and reflective learners they long to be.

4
Inclusion

> **Chapter Outline**
>
> Play for **All** children

'This is the only place where I can be me', Tia said about the play setting. Tia was nine and her childhood was at times difficult and challenging. Her mum was an alcoholic and Tia had shared with the playworkers that she felt like she had to tread on eggshells when she was at home, so as to not irritate and upset her mum; she had to be continuously alert to sense how to behave around her. Her dad worked long hours to support the family and experienced episodes of depression. He was frequently weary and sad, and Tia felt a need to care for him and look after him, such as making him cups of tea and making the family meals. Her twin sisters were ten years older than her and at college and spent most of their time with their friends rather than being at home. At school, Tia struggled to concentrate, she wanted to learn and make her mum and dad proud, but she found it very hard and was frequently in trouble for not paying attention. Tia felt that she had to take on different roles, sometimes these were coping methods just to get by and sometimes the roles were imposed on her by others because of their expectations of her. In the majority of environments that Tia spent her time in, she felt she had to try and be someone else, to please other people, to fit in, to be helpful, to meet other people's agendas; she felt she couldn't be herself. In the play setting, Tia could be herself, it was a place where she felt she belonged and was welcomed for who she was.

This example has been chosen to introduce some key ideas about the playwork approach and inclusion. Tia refers to the play setting as being the only place she feels she can be herself. This is something that does not *just happen*. Julia recalls many times when parents and other adults have looked around at a play setting where she has been working and commented on what an easy job it must be to be a playworker, to create and offer a space where all children can play; that it just involves opening up the space and letting them get on with it. It can appear deceptively easy, especially when you look across a setting and see children playing happily. However, as this chapter and subsequent chapters such as Chapter 5 and 6 will explore, co-creating an inclusive, personally safe and welcoming space where children can freely play, involves consideration of multiple different entangled aspects and much work behind the scenes to enable it to appear as if it 'just happens'.

Before we explore the entangled aspects that enabled the play setting to be a place in which Tia could be herself, let's take a moment to think about what the term 'inclusion' means for us. When you think of inclusion, what comes to mind? Do you think about including disabled children? Do you think about including children from diverse ethnic backgrounds and cultures? Or maybe you think of inclusion as welcoming all children and working towards developing settings in which all children feel like they truly belong (Douch 2020)? It can also be helpful to think about exclusion; what factors might exclude a child or young person or not make them feel welcome? What you think of as inclusion will be influenced by your previous experience, training and understanding. Reflecting on what we think and where our ideas have come from is important for developing our inclusive practice and our understanding.

Borkett (2018:12) suggests that inclusion 'is a much contested, multifaceted term, which has evolved over the years'. Having traditionally been used only about disabled children, it now applies to all areas of childhood. Savage (2015) suggests that there is no single way of looking at inclusion or thinking about it. He goes on to use the image of standing on a hilltop and being able to see the whole panorama but from the bottom of the hill only a fraction of the landscape is visible. To get the whole picture, it is necessary to walk around the hill, stopping and observing and then joining up the fragments. He suggests so it is with inclusion, that if we want to understand what inclusion means in practice, then we need to look at our practice from many different angles. The word 'inclusion' is open to different interpretations; it can mean being a part of something, it can emphasize *including* certain children and young people and it may be assumed that those being included are being included as equals, but are they? Including certain children and young people can also be viewed as implying a hierarchy, for example disabled children being seen as additional extras, being asked to join something that was established for non-disabled children. This frames disabled children as 'others' (Campbell 2009) in comparison with non-disabled children. As Kids (2006) point out having disabled children should not be seen as an optional extra to add on to a setting, it should be an inseparable part of the inclusive ethos which permeates throughout the whole setting. As will be explored later in this chapter, it needs to be a whole team approach, reflecting an attitude of mind that underpins the way in which everything is carried out. It should be the culture of the setting.

Over the years, Julia has worked in a variety of settings in different roles, such as a playworker in varied play settings with disabled and non-disabled children, teacher in primary schools, teaching assistant and volunteer in special schools and play support worker for a disabled young person. What she learnt was that inclusion means very different things in these different contexts and has different challenges for implementation. For example, in education settings, the pressure to achieve attainment targets and outcomes in order to demonstrate effectiveness may conflict with the desire to include disabled children if their inclusion is perceived as potentially lowering achievement levels (Ainscow, Booth and Dyson 2006). Ali recalls several schools that became academies in England where special needs coordinators (SENCOs) and/or pastoral staff were made redundant, and children had to be moved to other local schools – all due to the new management wanting to raise attainment levels.

So, what was the play setting offering Tia that she felt that it was a place, the only place of the different environments she was involved in that she could be herself? What does the playwork approach offer to understanding inclusion? There are key aspects of the playwork approach which differentiate it from other childhood services' approaches and inform its relationship to inclusion. These include its understanding of play and the way that playworkers interact with children and young people to support the play process. These key aspects help enable co-creating an inclusive space where children can play freely and be themselves.

The playwork approach's understanding of play is expressed in the Playwork Principles. Playwork Principle 1 (PPSG 2005) states, 'All children and young people need to play. The impulse to play is innate. Play is a biological, psychological and social necessity, and is fundamental to the healthy development and well-being of individuals and communities'. There has been debate about the use of the catch-all phrase 'all children' throughout the Playwork Principles as children are not a homogeneous group, they are not all the same. While this is true, it is also problematic to identify all groupings of children as this list could never be complete and would exclude. The term 'all children' was decided to be the most succinct and inclusive approach and is the term used in other children's rights documents such as the UN Convention on the Rights of the Child 1989 (Play Wales 2023). The playwork approach aims to flatten the hierarchy where certain children, such as disabled children, are viewed as additional extras. It recognizes that all children need to play and that many children, disabled and non-disabled, will for a variety of reasons experience barriers to playing freely and will need extra consideration given to enable them to participate as fully as they wish. This places a responsibility in the playwork approach to create environments that enable children and young people to play. This involves identifying and removing barriers, both physical and attitudinal, that get in the way of children being able to play. 'All children and young people' means **all** children and young people, not just some children and young people.

Playwork Principle 2 (PPSG 2005) also identifies how play is viewed in the playwork approach stating that 'Play is a process that is freely chosen, personally directed and intrinsically motivated. That is, children and young people determine and control the content and intent of their play, by following their own instincts, ideas and interests, in their own way for their own reasons'. This understanding of play emphasizes it as belonging to children, rather than as an activity that is given to them as something to do by adults and that children have choice and control over the content, intention and way they play. Within the playwork approach, play is not used by adults as a tool for learning or development. Learning and development may occur, but this is not the aim of the approach. Play is not used as a diagnostic tool to assess children's abilities, nor is it used to 'fix' children, which is a concern raised about the use of play in other childhood services by childhood disability studies authors such as Goodley and Runswick-Cole (2010). They argue that disabled children are often not allowed to *just* play; their play is frequently commandeered to fulfil an instrumental or diagnostic role, a sentiment shared in Natasha's reflection about playing with her disabled son, Arno.

> *I feel that right from birth playing with Arno was hijacked; it couldn't be play just for fun, it always seems like it has to have a purpose, like helping develop his senses or his social skills. Often it seems like a chore, not like play at all.*

Hodge and Runswick-Cole (2013) refer to the value of a space just to *be* for disabled children. Goodley and Runswick-Cole (2010) refer to the importance of leisure opportunities such as play involving children's *being* rather than *becoming*. What Goodley and Runswick-Cole (2010) are referring to in using the terms *being* and *becoming* are the frequently debated but still often dominant ideas about how children are viewed which subsequently can affect how their play is viewed and valued and what opportunities are made available or not available to them. Uprichard (2008) explains the *being* child as one who is viewed as a social actor, active in constructing their own everyday lived experiences, whereas the *becoming* child is seen as an adult in waiting, emphasizing what the child lacks in comparison with the adult they will become, rather than what they are in the current time. Play for the *being* child involves what Else (2014:20) refers to as the 'nowness' of play, play in the moment, which may have connections to previous play experiences, but may not and what it will lead on to or not lead on to is up to the child. It is their play that they are doing for its own sake because they want to play, they are the experts in being themselves and in their play. Whereas play for the *becoming* child may be restricted, as Natasha reflected, to only play that has a purpose, to aid development, correct problems and to fill in the gaps with the skills needed for becoming an adult. What are your thoughts about how children are viewed and how this might affect what opportunities for play are made available to them? Have you encountered these viewpoints? What do you think about play involving children's being rather than becoming? Do you think that play can involve both being and becoming?

From the playwork perspective, *all* children and young people should be able to play without there having to be an instrumental outcome. In recognizing play as being intrinsically motivated, the playwork perspective views play as being personal to the child, they play because they want to, they play for the sake of playing rather than for an end result and they control the choices they make about their play (Beunderman 2010). For Tia, this is what the play setting provided, a space where she could freely play and just *be*, there was no pressure to achieve outcomes unlike other childhood places (Goodley and Runswick-Cole 2010).

Another key aspect that distinguishes the playwork approach from other childhood services' approaches, which has an influence on inclusion, is the way in which playworkers interact with children and young people to support the play process. Roger Hart, a key researcher and author in children's participation, suggests that what is unique about the playwork approach is that, unlike other professions, playworkers work horizontally with children, that they work collaboratively with children rather than from a position of power (Play Wales 2008). The playwork approach focuses on playworkers operating by being in service to children, rather than being in charge of them. Playworkers work with the child's agenda, supporting their play rather than imposing external targets.

This flattens the traditional hierarchy of the power relations between adults and children and young people observed in other childhood services in which children and young people are viewed as subordinate to and dependent on adults (Wragg 2018). This links back to the idea of the *being* child rather than the *becoming* child mentioned previously in this chapter, as within the playwork approach, children and young people are valued for who they are in the here and now, not in anticipation of the potential adults they may become in the future. Wragg (2011) suggests that while the playwork approach does not go as far as thinking that children and young people should be afforded equal status to adults, children and young people are viewed as having equal value. Children's biological immaturity is acknowledged as making them more vulnerable than adults and therefore in need of greater rights of protection from themselves and others, but that this does not make them of less value. The flattened hierarchy of power relationships between playworkers and children and young people is one of the things that is unique about playwork and the most important aspect of playwork for developing children's sense of belonging, ownership and place where they can just *be* within a play setting. However, it is often one that many adults find the most uncomfortable to implement in practice initially, especially if they previously have worked in other childhood settings because they are so used to the power relations between adults and children and young people being imbalanced, with the adult being in a dominant position of being in control and in charge. What are your thoughts about the flattened hierarchy of power relationships between playworkers and children and young people? Is that something you can see the benefits of in terms of inclusion? Is it something that could be regularly practised in non-playwork settings?

The atmosphere of a setting is an important part of co-creating an inclusive, personally safe and welcoming space. We will at some point have felt the mood of a space, what Anderson (2014:136) refers to as the 'affective atmosphere'. Think about somewhere you have been to recently, it could be a supermarket, a friend's house or your work environment. What was the atmosphere like? How did the space feel? How did it make you feel? What was its mood? Atmospheres vary, they may be felt to be positive and welcoming, they may be felt to be negative, uncomfortable, awkward, claustrophobic or even frightening. They may have been felt as somewhere in between positive and negative or the mood of the space may have fluctuated. Multiple different entangled factors co-create an atmosphere and consequently, for those of us who work or are involved with children, understanding what creates an atmosphere is important.

A philosophical approach which can help us understand the multiple different entangled aspects involved in co-creating the atmosphere of a space is posthumanism. This approach involves flattening the hierarchy of all things as it views all things in a space as equally important, not just the humans. As an example of this, have a look at Figure 4.1. When we look at Figure 4.1, our eyes are probably first drawn to the young people. We tend to home in on people naturally first and then our eyes may drift to the wall and perhaps the sky, things that we view as being in the background. However, in the posthuman approach, all the 'things' are of equal value, nothing is designated to the background including sensory aspects such as the coldness of the wind, the brightness of the sunshine, the roughness of the individual bricks in the wall and the taste and smell of the sea in the air. Entangled with these aspects are also matterings, things that matter, that are important (Blundell 2016) such as the young people's thoughts, feelings and memories in relation to the space, each other, anyone else around and their sense of belonging.

Understanding how the different multi-sensory aspects and matterings entangle to become more than a sum of their separate parts and create the

Figure 4.1 Wall story. 2022. Courtesy of Sexton.

atmosphere of a setting can help us be more attuned to creating the conditions that can encourage an inclusive, welcoming atmosphere.

The playwork approach sometimes supports *all* children playing together, without any initial need for adult intervention, just because of the general inclusive atmosphere of a play setting, as the following example shows from Meriden Adventure Playground.

Children were jumping off a platform onto a deep crash mat, and one lad with Down's syndrome went up to see if he could do it. He 'ummed' and 'aahed' for quite a while with other kids saying things like – 'you can do it' and 'only try if you feel safe', and so on. He went to the back of the queue several times but kept standing on the edge and really wanting to. Eventually, he did and that whole end of the playground – all the children waiting to have a go and/or standing at the bottom – erupted into applause and shouts of 'yeah!' It was lovely to see and quite unprovoked . . .

However, as the title of *Kids'* (2006) inclusive management book emphasizes, 'It doesn't just happen' as the following reflection demonstrates.

Teresa, a playworker, recalls working in an after-school club located in a school building, which was staffed predominantly with childcare and nursery workers. Snack time at the after-school club was a social time when all the children sat down together and ate together with fruit in bowls placed on each table for the children to help themselves. The expectation was that all children would sit down and eat their snack happily together. Ella-Mai, an autistic child, attended the after-school club and found joining in with snack time difficult, for which she was often reprimanded sharply and loudly by some of the workers, which just increased her anxiety and distress. On occasions, this would lead to an escalation in what staff viewed as disruptive behaviour, and her mum would be called to collect her.

Teresa frequently had to intervene with a more playful and calm response to support Ella-Mai during snack time, but this response was frowned upon by other staff who felt that this was letting Ella-Mai 'get away' with misbehaving. There was an emphasis on staff managing the children's behaviour and children doing as they were told.

Through careful observation of Ella-Mai's behaviour and speaking with her mum, Teresa learnt that Ella-Mai had an intense dislike of stickers on fruit, which was often the case with the fruit in the bowls on the table at snack time. She also needed space and found being in close proximity to others uncomfortable, so being squashed together round a small snack table, she found very difficult to cope with. Teresa shared what she had found out with the staff team, but this was dismissed as Ella-Mai just being fussy and awkward.

One worker commented 'there's nothing wrong with her, she is just being naughty and I'm not having it'.

What are your thoughts about this reflection? What would you have done in this situation? How would you have viewed Ella-Mai's behaviour? What do you think the adult's role is here? Is it to be in charge, manage the children's behaviour and make sure they all do as they are told? Should Ella-Mai fit in with everyone else? Would you have tried a playful calm response to support Ella-Mai at snack time? Once you knew that Ella-Mai had an intense dislike for stickers on fruit, would you have found the time to remove them before putting them out at snack time? Or would you have thought she was just being fussy and should get used to them? Knowing that Ella-Mai found being in close proximity to others uncomfortable, would you have thought about how to change the table layout or perhaps considered alternative ways to have snack to provide more space for everyone? Disabled children are not a homogenous group and include children with a wide range of impairments (Kids 2006). Do you think autistic children may be responded to differently than disabled children with more visually apparent impairments? What could be done to support Ella-Mai feel how Tia feels about the play setting she attends, that she belongs and is welcomed for who she is and it is a place where she can be herself?

The reflection raises some interesting questions about how adults view and understand inclusion and the different factors affecting it. The comment by the worker 'there's nothing wrong with her, she is just being naughty and I'm not having it' is especially revealing. What do they mean by 'there's nothing wrong with her'? The words we use, which will be discussed later in this chapter, are important because of the messages they give out. By using the word 'wrong' does the worker mean an impairment, indicating that the worker views disability from the medical model of disability? The medical model of disability considers a disabled person in medical terms, focusing on their impairments, views these as things that are 'wrong' with the individual in comparison with having a normative body, as a deficit rather than an aspect of human diversity (Huang and Brittain 2006) and in need of fixing. Whereas the social model of disability emphasizes the barriers that are created for disabled people; how the physical environment creates barriers for access and how attitudes exclude disabled people from full participation in society, rather than individual impairment (Goble and Bye-Brooks 2016). Disability is understood to be caused predominantly by society's responses to people's impairments rather than the impairments themselves. Does the worker's comments indicate that if they thought there was something 'wrong' with Ella-Mai, then they would respond differently to her behaviour? Is the worker even aware that Ella-Mai is autistic? This also raises the question about whether Ella-Mai's parents had the opportunity when submitting contact details and registration information for her to attend the after-school club, to include information to enable the playworkers to meet her needs most effectively and if they did, then has this been shared with all staff?

The comment 'I'm not having it' identifies the view the worker has of the power relationships between the adults and the children in the setting, that the adult is in charge. However, the playwork approach focuses on playworkers operating by being in service to children, and working co-operatively with them, rather than being in charge of them. This enables playworkers to empower children in different ways (Play Wales 2008). This also relates to the ideas of playworkers co-creating space with children that are explored further in Chapter 5, such as the ideas of open and closed spaces referred to by Lester (2008). In open spaces, diversity and difference are valued whereas in closed spaces everyone in them is expected to adhere to the adult-established norms and values. Do you think that the after-school club being located in a school building had an effect on the power relationships between the adults and the children? Do you think they might have been different if the after-school club was located outside of the school? How are difference and diversity valued where you work? Do you think that having staff with qualifications and experience from different childhood settings, such as nurseries and childcare settings, makes a difference to the power relationships between the adults and the children in the after-school club? As a previous senior playwork colleague of Julia's once said, 'if a mouse is in a stable, does that make it a horse? And if an employee is in a play setting, does that make them a playworker?'

This leads us to think about the importance of all staff, despite, or perhaps because of their potentially diverse experiences and qualifications, being fully informed of what they need to know to support all the children, help make them feel welcome, and for staff to feel confident in doing so. That for inclusion to happen, it needs to be a whole team approach, as the next reflection shows.

Julia recalls visiting a children's centre when she noticed a disabled child who was a wheelchair user frantically making the Makaton (a language programme that uses symbols, signs and speech to enable people to communicate) *sign for 'toilet' and looking very distressed. The staff in the room were busy, but a staff member went over to the child and asked verbally if she* was ok but didn't seem to understand what the child was trying to communicate and moved away. At that time one of Julia's jobs involved working with a disabled young person who used Makaton to communicate, so she was very familiar with that sign. She caught the eye of a staff member as she went over to the child, verbally saying and signing in Makaton 'you need the toilet?' The child looked relieved and frantically started signing 'yes!' 'yes!' 'yes!' The staff member looked surprised and swiftly helped the child get to the toilet. Later on, the same staff member asked if that was what the sign meant as she had seen it done before but didn't know what it meant. Julia explained that it was the Makaton sign for toilet and started to rummage in her bag for a copy of her Makaton signage guide to give to the staff member. She was interrupted by a senior worker who said it was fine, they didn't need the signage guide because there was already one in the main office. Julia politely suggested that it would be a good idea if every staff member had a copy and training in Makaton so they could confidently communicate with all the children.

An important part of inclusion is children and young people having a voice, being able to make decisions and having their say. For children and young people who do not use verbal communication, they need multiple methods to be able to have their say. What opportunities do you provide for children to have their say? And can you be sure that these opportunities do not 'lead' children to say what they think you want to hear rather than what they really think?

In addition to practical information for supporting children and young people's communication, it is important for all staff to have a shared understanding of play to enable co-creating a space where children and young people can play. In relation to this, Idris recalls his first day working on a summer playscheme for disabled children located in a special school.

In the hall, several children who used wheelchairs were sitting in a circle; trays had been attached across the front of their wheelchairs, and various toys had been placed on the trays for the children to play with. As I walked across the hall towards the children, Asim looked up at me and pushed one of his toys off his tray and looked back at me. I took this to be a play cue, that Asim was signalling that he wanted to play with me, so I picked up the toy with a flourish, held it up saying 'Aha' and plonked it down on Asim's tray on top of another toy. Asim looked at the toy, then pushed the toy and the one underneath it off his tray and looked at me again, with what I thought was a hint of a smile. A teacher passed by and saw what was going on. She swiftly picked up the toys, put them firmly back on the tray, and said to me, 'Try and keep the toys on the tray, will you?' I jokingly said to Asim, 'Ooh, you've got me in trouble now and on my first day too', to which the teacher didn't laugh or tell me off for being cheeky but said, 'Do you speak Hindi?', to which I said, 'no'. She tutted and said, 'Well, he', nodding towards Asim 'won't be able to understand you, will he?" and walked away. Feeling a bit awkward, unintentionally (or maybe intentionally?), I rolled my eyes and pulled a funny face while looking at Asim who started laughing and frantically pushing all the toys off his tray as quickly as he could. I laughed and picked them up one at a time, placing each one again with a playful flourish onto Asim's tray, to which he pushed them all off again. This game continued with much laughter from both of us until we were told it was time to put away the toys as it was snack time. Another member of staff who had heard my conversation with the teacher and seen me playing with Asim came over and said, 'I don't know about the international language of play, but I do know that is the first time I have seen Asim laugh and have so much fun'.

From a playwork perspective, Asim issues a play cue (Sturrock and Else 1998), a signal he wants to play by looking at Idris, pushing one of his toys off his tray and then looking back at him. Idris interprets this as a play cue and responds by picking up the toy with a flourish, holds it up saying 'Aha' and plonks it down on Asim's tray on top of another toy. Idris makes a playful response with exaggerated actions. The aim of his response is to support Asim's play, not replace it with his own adult actions (Else 2014). However, not everyone will recognize these cues as signals to play. They may miss seeing them at all, misunderstand them or recognize them as signals to play but ignore them because they feel it is not the right time to play or not the right time for a particular sort of play. This may be the case with the teacher in the example when she picks up the toys and puts them back on the tray. Both Idris and the teacher put toys back on the tray after Asim has pushed them off. Idris's playful response opens up the possibilities for supporting Asim's play, the teacher's response appears more focused on keeping things neat and tidy. It is also interesting that the teacher mentions Asim's home language of Hindi being a barrier for Asim to understand Idris, when play was being used by Idris and Asim as a method of communication. While it is very beneficial to have community languages spoken by staff in settings, the lack of this should not be used as an excuse to exclude children. Alternative methods can be used, such as all staff learning key words and remembering all the different ways that children communicate, not just through speech, such as through eye-gazing, pointing, drawing and through play. Children often play successfully together without a common language. How would you have responded to Asim?

An example of a play organization working together to develop a child's sense of belonging is shown in the following example.

Many of the children and families who use Pitsmoor Adventure Playground are new migrants from diverse backgrounds who have experienced disruption and uncertainty in their lives. English is frequently not their first language, and they face barriers to becoming settled in the area. The key to developing children's sense of belonging and empowerment is to make them feel welcome and valued. Staff at the playground take time to get to know children and their families, showing a genuine interest and building positive and respectful relationships. Staff speak a range of community languages and have an understanding of different cultural traditions.

Sufian, aged seven years, and his extended family were introduced to the playground by Early Help staff. He had arrived in the UK from an area of war and conflict as a child asylum seeker and had recently joined his extended family in Sheffield after being separated from his family in Yemen. He was a very withdrawn and frightened child and was malnourished. The playground provided him with a safe haven to be a child, to play, explore and learn. His English skills have increased through play and he has been able to communicate with an Arabic-speaking playworker at the playground. His inclusion into the Yemeni and multicultural community in the area has been made markedly easier by his being one of the 'Pitsmoor Adventure Playground children' which has in turn helped him to integrate in school, according to teachers' and Early Help workers' reports. He is flourishing physically and emotionally and is always one of the first at the gate after school to come into the playground.

As touched on earlier, the language we use is important. You will have noticed that we have referred to disabled children rather than children with disabilities throughout this chapter. Referring to disabled children uses identity-first language, whereas children with disabilities uses person-first language. Using identity-first language reflects the preferences of many disabled people and aligns with the social model of disability (Hansen, Bialka and Wong 2022). However, while we use identity-first language, it is important to recognize that this is not the preferred approach for all disabled people. The same words can be viewed as appropriate in one country and inappropriate in another. For example, Bozalek and Fullagar (2022) note that they use the word 'disabled' in their chapter Able/Disabled for a UK audience as UK activists emphasize the social model of disability, people being disabled by environments. Whereas in Australia, the term 'disabled person' is viewed as a negative term and person with disabilities is preferred. A key aspect of inclusive practice is that it is important to remember that words matter and using appropriate language is more than just trying to be politically correct, it is about thinking about what message our words give out. Using the right terms can feel like a minefield and we can be tempted to avoid using any terms at all for fear of getting it wrong and upsetting people. To inform our inclusive practice, we need to be mindful of how the children, young people and families we are involved with identify themselves. For example, many deaf people whose first language is British Sign Language (BSL) describe themselves as 'Deaf', with a capital D, to emphasize their deaf identity (GOV.UK 2021) but others may prefer to identify with having a hearing impairment. We need to reflect on whether our choice of words emphasizes children and young people as active individuals with control over their own lives, or if they emphasize passivity and deficits.

In this chapter, we have explored using the playwork approach in order to include children and give them the freedom to be themselves. Wherever we work with children and in whatever setting, it is possible to use this non-hierarchical approach in order to better understand and support children and recognize that playing is the main way they communicate. Do you agree?

5
Space, Environment and the Outdoors

Chapter Outline
Co-creating space for play

A popular way to begin playwork training is to get the participants to remember their childhoods, often asking them what, where and when they played and with whom. When asked about where he played, Simon, thinking back to his childhood in the 1970s, recalled a favourite place, a tree.

When I was about seven or eight years old, one game I would regularly play with a couple of friends was 'World War II Bomber crew'. This took place at a lightning split tree we called 'the bomber' for obvious reasons. This tree was located in a field near my house. We would walk across the field to the bomber and then climb it. I was the least comfortable with heights, and so I would climb to a space in the bomber about six feet off the ground. The other two would usually climb higher; the unofficial rules were that whoever climbed highest was the captain and pilot, next down was the machine gunner and finally (usually me) was the navigator. We only played this game in 'the bomber'; the tree was our plane. There was a playground about 10 minutes' walk away, with slides and climbing frames, but we played different games there; without that specific tree, we couldn't play that specific game.

Simon's reflection will be used to introduce several key points about space, the environment, the outdoors and playwork. First, when Simon is asked to think of where he played, he recalls a favourite *place*, a tree, and refers to climbing into the *space* created by the tree's split. It might seem a bit pedantic to focus on the use of these different words, but do we mean different things when we refer to *places* rather than *spaces*? Or do we use the words interchangeably? Does it matter? If we are involved in thinking about creating spaces for play, then what we understand play and space to be (and what the other people we work with understand them to be) may matter a great deal.

As a term, *space* can be ambiguous as it can have numerous meanings and various interpretations (Harvey 2009). James and James (2012) suggest that space and place are different concepts, but that there is a close relationship between them. For many authors, *space* refers to the physical qualities of an area, whereas *place* is more than this. Spaces become places through the interactions that occur within them, their social and cultural meanings (Hammond 2003). Therefore, in Simon's reflection, 'the bomber' is a *place*, it becomes so because of the interactions of Simon and his friends climbing on it and using it for their game, through which it acquires social and cultural meanings. In addition, Tuan (1974) suggests that *place* has two meanings which can overlap and be entangled. It can describe a spatial location, such as 'the bomber' in Simon's reflection, but it can also describe someone's position in society, for example, 'being put in your place' or 'knowing your place.' In relation to Simon's reflection, this might have occurred if an adult had intervened, stopping the children's play in the tree because they felt it was not a place for children to be playing. They might have told the children to go and play somewhere else such as the playground, the place that adults have designated as the place for children's play. Hatton (2024) refers to the *space* of childhood, where children have their own space in society, created by social and political constructions of childhood and by their creation of sub-cultures through their play and cultural interests. Fog Olwig and Gulløv (2003) reflect on what messages the physical spaces adults design and designate to children and young people give out about children and young people's place in society. For example, keeping them separate from adults but still observable (Opie and Opie 1969) and emphasizing their difference or 'otherness' to adults. What do the terms space and place mean to you?

Spencer and Blades (2006) explore the different types of spaces where children and young people play. They differentiate between spaces *for* children, which are those spaces designed by adults for children such as schools, nurseries, play centres, playgrounds, and spaces *of* children, which are spaces children create for themselves. In Simon's reflection, he refers to both a space *for* children, the playground with its slide and climbing frames, and a space *of* children, 'the bomber', the tree that he and his friends made into their own space, which in their play became a plane. In this space, they negotiated their own rules, such as whoever climbed the furthest got to have the highest ranking role.

Figure 5.1 Me and my friends go under the coats. 2018. Courtesy of Kellock and Sexton.

Spaces *of* children will often occur within spaces *for* children, for example, children creating a den under the coat pegs in a primary school classroom (Figure 5.1). This image is from Kellock and Sexton's (2018) research into children's perspectives on their school space. It was taken by Tom, a child in year four, who identified this as a space he had made for himself and his friends even though (or perhaps because) playing under the coats was against the school rules as this space was not a designated play area (Kellock and Sexton 2018).

They also may occur in spaces that are not primarily designed for children, for example, in a supermarket, as Julia's reflection below demonstrates.

I was shopping in a large supermarket, looking at a rail of clothes when as I moved a shirt forward, a child, aged about six's face appeared from beneath the clothes rail. The child stood up, spread out their arms and smiled up at me. 'Welcome to my shop' they said, stepping out from the clothes rail, twirling around with their arms outstretched. 'What would you like to buy?' I told them I was looking for some pyjamas. They grinned, 'Excellent! Follow me, I'll take you to them. I have lots in my shop' and they proceeded to push some clothes on the clothes rail to one side and duck underneath.

These examples raise some interesting thoughts for those of us who work or are involved with children and young people in relation to our understanding of play and space. They refer to physical spaces, the outdoors, a classroom and a supermarket, but they also reveal entangled aspects that create the space; the interactions within the space both with other people and with things, as well as intangible aspects such as a sense of belonging and playfulness. Simon's reflection and Tom's photograph refer to play spaces that have been created by children with no adult involvement. Ward (1979) stated children will play everywhere and with anything and the Opies (1969:10) exploring the games children play outdoors, suggested that 'where children are is where they play'. If these statements are true, and as some of the previous examples have shown, children will play in different spaces and create their own spaces of play without adult involvement. What do you think? If children can do this without adults, what role can adults have?

Playwork Principle 5 (PPSG 2005) states that 'The role of the playworker is to support all children and young people in the creation of a space in which they can play' but what does this mean in practice? Playworkers work with children and young people in a wide range of settings, such as adventure playgrounds, out-of-school provision, play buses, play projects, play ranger projects, schools, hospitals, refuges and prisons (Russell 2010). Consequently, they work in a diverse range of spaces, including different kinds of buildings and outdoor areas.

These spaces will be spaces *for* children, even if they are spaces *for* children created within spaces for adults, such as a children's space within a prison. The purpose of these types of provision may vary; it may not be to provide spaces for play; it may be to provide childcare for parents, or education or healthcare. Many of these spaces will be shared spaces such as an after-school club located within a primary school, or a play ranger project located in a local park, and these can bring additional potential challenges when trying to support children and young people in creating spaces in which they can play. These challenges may involve shared use, limited time, storage, resources, layout of rooms and buildings, different perspectives on play and different agendas which can all impact on creating a sense of identity and ownership.

As the example from Jacky in Chapter 1 about running an out-of-school club described, responding to these types of challenges requires careful negotiation of the space and some aspects may be outside of our control and instead require compromise and developing creative, flexible responses.

Over the years that Julia has been a playworker, she has worked in numerous different environments and all of these, apart from two, have been in shared or borrowed spaces; spaces *for* children such as school buildings and also spaces not specifically designed for children, like community centres. Both of these types of spaces can raise challenges for creating a space in which children can play, as the following reflections will show, let alone thinking about what it means to *support* all children and young people in the creation of a space in which they can play.

For many playworkers, like Julia's reflection below shows, the space that has been provided requires action to create it into a space in which children can play.

I remember working in a holiday club one summer for children aged five to twelve years which was located in the ground floor rooms of a nursery. The furniture was designed for children under five, so it was much too small for the children attending the playscheme. There were also a lot of toys and equipment set out that the nursery staff told us we weren't allowed to use, and we couldn't move elsewhere out of the way. The manager of the nursery had agreed to host the holiday club in their setting but hadn't realized that changes would need to take place to make it a suitable space for play for the age and size of the children who would be attending. Some quick thinking, lots of negotiation and scavenging for different resources were needed to create a space where the children could play.

In addition, Idris's reflection below shows how a space that is not designed for children can have great potential as a space for play but how another adult's view on space can impact on this.

I remember working in a summer playscheme which was located in a community centre. We had access during the day to the whole building and the back doors opened out onto large playing fields. We had a great physical space to play with. However, it came with a caretaker who disapproved of the building being used by 'messy children, making my life a misery' who would come to inspect 'his' building every evening and make me, as senior playworker, walk round with him so he could point out any smudge of paint on a table or a fingerprint on a window. He viewed the community centre very much as his space, and the playwork team and the children spent the summer negotiating co-creating the play space with him.

Idris's reflection introduces the idea of space being negotiated and co-created, rather than being actively created by adults for children to passively use. When we look closely, we notice that Playwork Principle 5 states that 'The role of the playworker is to **support** all children and young people in the creation of a space in which they can play' which is subtly different to just creating a space *for* children in which they can play; it brings together the ideas of spaces *for* and *of* children. This indicates co-creation in which playworkers, children and young people and, as we will explore further later in this chapter, things create the space together with the playworker taking a supportive role.

This Playwork Principle is open to interpretation and can prompt playworkers to review their practice. Julia recalls visiting an after-school club which was run in a community hall and observing the children being greeted warmly by the playworkers as they arrived, but that the hall itself was empty, with just the back cupboards being open. In these cupboards, the furniture, such as the tables and chairs, and all the other resources were kept. The children were busy getting out what they wanted from the cupboards. If they needed help getting something out, they called over a playworker to help. The coordinator explained that when she first started working at the club as a playworker, she just fitted in with the usual routine. This had involved setting out tables with certain activities, such as arts and crafts activities on a couple of tables, board games on another, putting bean bags and large cushions for chilling out on in a corner of the hall, and perhaps some large boxes or things that the playworkers thought might interest the children. As she was also a teaching assistant in a school, she was familiar with setting out activities for children, and as the children always seemed to find something to play with, she did not give this much thought.

However, when she started some playwork training and learnt about the Playwork Principles, she began to think about what was meant by supporting children in creating a space in which they could play. She started to wonder if she was just creating a space that she thought the children would like to play in. Over the next few years, she kept thinking about this and trying different things, and gradually the staff team started to do things differently. They don't put anything out for the children, the children get out what they want, often bringing in things themselves. She explained the role of the playworkers as being like stagehands, providing the props or set pieces that are needed. The children start with a blank canvas, an empty hall, and then find what they need from the cupboards, and the playworkers' roles are to help support them to do that. Changing previous habits and routines took time and required getting playworkers, children and parents/carers on board. Some of the playworkers found not setting out activities and preparing the room difficult, as they felt that was their role and that they should be in charge of what was put out. Parents and carers also questioned what the playworkers were actually doing if they were not setting up things for the children to do. The coordinator shared that one dad had jokingly asked if it was a 'do it yourself' after-school club. It had also taken time for the children to adjust, as they were used to having things provided for them and some were daunted by having more choice and freedom.

This recollection identifies issues with the distribution of power and control between playworkers and children in relation to creating spaces for children to play. These ideas resonate with the findings of Smith and Barker's (2000) study into play in after-school provision, which found that most play activities were planned by adult staff. Depending on the setting, staff may feel they need to justify the play and that their role should focus on learning outcomes, rather than supporting the play process (King and Newstead 2022). Lester (2008), referring to the work of Sibley, explored the ideas of open and closed spaces. A closed space is one which is a defined space where there are established boundaries, norms and values, with an expectation that everyone involved in the space will adhere to these. In relation to the after-school club just mentioned, when adults' values were imposed on the children, through adults feeling that their role was to be in charge of what resources were put out for the children and how they set out the space, this was a closed space. In contrast, open space is a more fluid space, in which difference and diversity are valued. These are spaces which 'provide a site of possibilities and ambiguity' (Lester 2008:55). In relinquishing control over what was put out for the children and not planning the activities, a more open space with more opportunities and possibilities was created.

Knowing how to respond when supporting children and young people's play can be challenging; we may personally find the play makes us feel uncomfortable, it may explore distressing themes, may be risky or we may be questioned by others about what we are or are not doing. A tool that can help reflect on our responses, both our actions and our feelings is Brawgs continuum, a model developed by Wendy Russell and informed by Arthur Battram and Gordon Sturrock; Brawgs being an anagram of the authors' initials (Brown, Long and Wragg 2018). Brawgs continuum presents a range of playwork responses. At one end of the continuum is the didactic (intended to teach) response in which the adult is directive, controlling the children's use of time, space and resources and making decisions on behalf of the child.

At the other end is the chaotic response in which the adult's responses to the children are unpredictable, resources are poorly maintained and the setting's opening times may be erratic. Both these ends of the continuum emphasize adults' needs; societal in the didactic response and personal in the chaotic response rather than those of the playing children and young people. The ludocentric (play-centred) response is located between these; here the responses support children and young people's play rather than other adult agendas (Russell 2008). Reflecting on where our responses are on the continuum at different times can enable us to be more aware of how our behaviour and feelings influence how we support children and young people's play and how we might work towards more frequently using a ludocentric response. What do you think about this way of supporting children in creating a space in which they can freely play?

The coordinator in the recollection refers to the role of the playworkers as being like stagehands, providing what props are needed. This relates to how Lester (2008) suggests playworkers should appreciate children's play as a performance, and the adult-created play space is the theatrical space or stage. When thinking about children's play and the play space in this way, the playworker's role in planning is about preparing the space for play, such as considering the layout and the resources within it and preparing themselves for having a supportive role in children's play, rather than planning play *for* children by rigidly organizing activities. Extending the theme of children's play as a performance and adult-created play spaces as theatrical spaces, Lester (2008) explores the role of playworkers within this, suggesting that the 'character' of the playworker is developed through a reflective role which may include:

- Rehearsals – recapturing the spirit of playfulness and recognizing the nature and purpose of playwork; using memory and imagination – using memories of playing, both as adults and children in the play space as an empathetic process.
- Prologues – playworkers talking together prior to the session, to establish the overall feel of the space and attuning to the children's current play experiences.
- Scene setters – through playworkers' understanding of play and spaces *for* and *of* children, this leads playworkers to consider what props may be needed to support the play and open up possibilities.
- Observation – using observation to gain impressions of the play.
- Prompts and provocations – through attuning to children's play, the playworker can identify when their role may be to intervene to support

play that has become destructive or unhelpfully stuck for a child or children.
- Epilogues and postscripts – playworkers reflecting on thoughts and feelings generated from the children's play and re-examining their actions and the impact of these.

Thinking about the adult's role in supporting children in creating spaces to play, Jacky recalls two examples in which different adults were involved in creating a den with a child, Alice, aged seven.

Alice was given a den-building kit for her birthday. This consisted of short poles that can be linked together in a whole range of different ways and a large covering with potential windows and different fastenings. The structure can be adapted into a variety of configurations. Alice and her mother began building the den together in a basement family room. The instructions were consulted, and the den was built in one of the ways suggested by them. There was the feeling that there was a 'right' or 'wrong' way to build the den. They did create a stable structure with an official tent-like feel to it, and Alice was happy making it cozy inside. She played in it with her friends – it was like camping.

Some months later, a playworker visited Alice's home, and Alice asked her if she would help her build a den. Alice got the kit out and a load of blankets, cushions and odds and ends. The playworker asked Alice what she wanted her to do, and Alice instructed her as to where she wanted the den and suggested using a wall, a folding gym mat, a cupboard and the edge of a sofa as part of the construction and asked the playworker to fit some poles together to make the rest of the edges and support for the roof. Alice was giving orders and organizing how the inside would be. If something was not working well, the playworker would tell Alice, and they would discuss what could be done instead. There was much experimentation, laughter and sometimes parts of the den would fall down. Eventually, a ramshackle set-up was put together and the covering was draped over as much as it would cover. Alice wrote a notice and stuck it on the outside of the door to the room that the den was in, to tell people not to enter as they might walk into a den. The playworker left Alice happily sorting her den out. The following day, the playworker returned to Alice's home, and the den now had further sheets and curtains pegged onto it to make it totally private. The playworker was invited inside to see how it looked. She had to crawl in. Various bits had been designated different rooms – kitchen, bathroom, living room and bedroom – only imagination would allow you to know which was which, but Alice was very happy and had had two friends playing in it the previous evening.

Both of these examples involve an adult and child creating a den together and demonstrate subtle and not so subtle differences in the adult's approaches to doing this. Both experiences offer learning opportunities and the different approaches taken by the adults impact on the benefits of these for Alice. From building with her mother, Alice would have learnt the importance of following instructions and how to build a stable construction – the instrumental value of play (Powell 2009) where play is viewed as having particular beneficial outcomes. This would have given her a sense of satisfaction. She was very happy with the den and will have played any number of things inside it, with and without her friends. From an educational perspective, the experience of building a den with her mother was a valuable tool for learning (Jarvis, Brock and Brown 2019). It offered Alice first-hand experiences to develop her thinking and learning, through handling the materials (Bruner 1966), working out how they connect together and watching her mother. From a developmental perspective, this offered an opportunity to develop cognitive, creative and physical skills, such as hand-to-eye coordination and problem-solving. Within this perspective, den-building is viewed as contributing to Alice's current and future competence, which is beneficial for her and that of society (Jarvis, Brock and Brown 2019). The process of creating the den together was in a structured and organized manner, rather than a playful, experimental experience. As such, it was like following instructions to build a flat-packed item of furniture, which is a useful skill for the future. Only once it is created does Alice have the opportunity to customize it by 'making it cosy inside' and playing in it with her friends.

The role of Alice's mother might be regarded as offering 'guided participation' (Rogoff 1990:111), giving instructions during a joint activity in which the outcome of creating a stable den according to the instructions is achieved. It also relates to the ideas of power and control between adults and children in relation to creating spaces for children to play previously mentioned in this chapter. The presence of particular people such as an adult, a playworker or child can sometimes be the catalyst for turning somewhere, not designated for play, into a space for play. For example, the atmosphere may change when a particular playful person arrives or starts playing. In both of the previous examples with Alice, the presence of an adult and their way of interacting with her during the den-building affected the atmosphere, the *feel* of the space. The first example mentions there being an atmosphere, a feeling that there was a 'right' or 'wrong' way to build the den. In the second example, a different atmosphere is created which is playful, involving experimentation and laughter.

From a playwork perspective, where the intrinsic value of play is recognized and play is valued in relation to children's enjoyment (Powell 2009), building a free-form den would have offered more opportunities for creative, exploratory and object play (Hughes 1996, 2006, 2012). Creative play enables children to explore materials for its own sake (Hughes 2012). Mastery play is about trying things out, involving trial and error (Hughes 2012). Exploratory play involves working with loose parts, working with materials to find out how they work (Hughes 2012). Object play involves children problem-solving and experimenting with the properties of objects and materials (Hughes 2012). Else (2014) suggests that for something to be play, it needs to involve choice, engagement and satisfaction. In the first example, Alice appears to have limited choice in how to create her den as the instructions are followed to create a den in one of the ways the instructions suggest; there is no improvisation. Being able to create the den how she wanted would have offered more opportunities for her to think for herself. It would have enabled her to experience being in charge and through experimenting with the materials for herself would have facilitated playing with uncertainty (Spinka, Newberry and Bekoff 2001), experiencing success and failure, and developing self-determination and perseverance.

The playwork approach focuses on supporting the play process (PPSG 2005). In the second example, the power dynamics between Alice and the playworker are very different. Alice asked the playworker if they would help her build a den, verbally she was issuing a play cue, a signal that she wanted to play. It was Alice who got the kit and additional items out and it was the playworker who asked Alice what she wanted them to do, and it was Alice who instructed, gave orders and organized how the inside of the den should be. This gave Alice the opportunity to be in charge and the playworker's role was like that of a stagehand, rather than directing the experience. Stagehands remain in the wings, only entering the stage to set the scene and then retreating to the wings when not needed, unobtrusively observing. The playworker fitted the den together, let Alice know if something did not work and they discussed together what else could be done. Once the den was created, the playworker left Alice to happily sort out her den. The playworker knew when they were no longer required to help support the play process and co-create the play space. The written instructions for how to build a den, which came with the kit, were not followed. There was no sense of a right or wrong way to create the den. A den was created, a 'ramshackle set up' which was Alice's space, which she later continues to develop. The process of making the den was playful, full of experimentation, in contrast with the first example, where the process of making the den was a means to an end. Example one lacked flexibility, relating to the closed space referred to by Lester (2008) mentioned earlier, whereas example two relates to the open space, a more fluid, flexible space with increased potential possibilities. How would you have created a den with Alice? Why?

Blundell (2016:45) refers to traditional ideas about space which view it as just a physical container as the 'dolls' house approach', where all the rooms are ready, and the adults' role is just to furnish them. A theory that can help extend our thinking about space and re-examine taken-for-granted assumptions is Lefebvre's (1991) Triad spatial theory. Lefebvre's theory aims to make sense of space, going beyond just focusing on the physical space to explore the cultural and everyday uses of such spaces to understand how spaces are produced (Jeyasingham 2013). Although Lefebvre (1991) refers to play in his work, his Triad theory was not specifically designed to examine play spaces. However, it has been used by playwork authors such as Russell (2012, 2018) and Lester (2020) to deepen understanding about play spaces such as adventure playgrounds and Delorme (2018) to analyse children's play experience.

In the Triad theory, Lefebvre (1991) identifies three interconnected and entangled aspects that produce space: the conceived space, perceived space and lived space. He also explores how the concept of time affects space. The conceived space is the planned space, what the space was designed for. This relates to the previously mentioned idea of spaces for children, spaces designed by adults for children. In relation to the variety of spaces in which playwork occurs, understanding this aspect can be very helpful, especially when it occurs in borrowed or shared spaces. For example, in an earlier reflection, Julia referred to working in a holiday club which was located in the ground floor rooms of a nursery. Understanding the conceived space, what this space was designed for, helps to understand why the space was problematic for running a holiday club for children aged five to twelve years. It was problematic because it was not designed to be used for that purpose. It was designed as an early childhood learning environment which influenced the size and layout of the room's furniture and the toys and equipment within that space and how the space should function. Have you encountered a space that was being used in a way that it wasn't designed for? Did this cause problems?

The perceived space is what is expected to happen within the space, the daily routines and practices, such as the type of relationships that develop within it over time. This again is very pertinent for playworkers to be aware of as Idris's reflection on working in a summer playscheme located in a community centre showed. This identified different perceptions about what should be happening in the space, the caretaker's and Idris's. The caretaker's view was that the community centre should not be used by children, this was not what had previously happened, and this was not what he expected to happen in this space. Previous routines and habits were disrupted, new people including children were using the space that the caretaker had to interact with. 'Mess' had been brought into the space through arts and crafts materials being used in the building, such as paint, and children touching things like the windows and leaving fingerprints. Whereas Idris (and the children) were expecting to use the space as a play space. Have you encountered different views on how a space should be used? How did you resolve this?

The third element of Lefebvre's (1991) Triad theory is the lived space, which comprises of intangible aspects such as the feel of the space, what actually happens in the space and how it is really used. These aspects may be very different from how the space was intended to be used by the designer. As referred to in Chapter 4, the feel of the space is what Anderson (2014:136) refers to as the 'affective atmosphere', one that is charged with emotional aspects that are difficult to put into words but can be sensed. The lived space is also produced through the relationships that occur within it, such as friendships, the emotional attachment to the space, a sense of belonging or of not belonging and the meaning the space holds for individuals. This relates to the idea of spaces of children, where children create their own spaces, often disrupting adults' notions of how the space should be used, causing tensions between the perceived space and the lived space as the example below shows.

The Weekenders is a community children's group and has the use of a church hall and adjoining rooms. During the week, these rooms are used by another community group, a group for disabled young people. Although the two groups have never met, some tensions related to the shared use of the space have been expressed through the leaving of notes. For example, notes telling the other group not to touch their stuff.

There is a staircase which leads from the ground floor main room to the upper rooms. At the top of the stairs is a large box which contains toys and on top of this box is a dolls' house with figures. Midway up the staircase, on the wall is a ledge. While creating artwork for a local children's art exhibition, two children from the Weekenders placed their paintings on this ledge. When they returned the next weekend, the paintings had been removed from the ledge and put in the main hall and several of the toys from the toy

Figure 5.2 Toys on the ledge. 2020. Courtesy of Sexton.

box had been placed on the ledge (Figure 5.2). Children from the Weekenders put the paintings back and added more toys. For three weeks this pattern continued. The week of the art exhibition, the paintings were taken to the exhibition space. The ledge remained free of any objects for several months. Then one weekend, the Weekenders found the ledge crowded with toys again, far more than had ever been put on there before. In addition, one wooden toy had been placed on a different ledge about eight-foot-high up on a wall and other toys had been positioned in random places, such as on the backs of chairs in the corridor outside the upper rooms.

This was noticed by the room-booking officer while bringing down tables and donations from the upper room for a tabletop sale. They tutted and looked disapproving and said 'That'll have to be stopped. Who's done that? That'll fall on someone's head if we're not careful'.

The concept of time can also be applied to understand how space evolves over time. For example, its use may change over time during the day. A school hall may be used for PE in the morning, requiring the PE equipment to be set out. It may be used as a dining hall during lunchtime, requiring tables and chairs to be set up, plates, cutlery and food to be brought in. It may then used for drama lessons in the afternoon, requiring a stage to be set up and various props to be brought in. After school, it may be used by an after-school club that sets up the hall out with various tables, chairs and other resources and equipment for play. There are different expectations for how the space is used, its function and how the children will behave for all these different activities. Considering the entangled aspects of conceived, perceived, lived space, and the effect of time can help deepen understanding of what it is like to experience play spaces and the adult's role within it.

For those of us who work or are involved with children, understanding what creates the atmosphere in a space is important. To help understand the different aspects that co-create, let's look at a photograph taken at Pitsmoor Adventure Playground (Figure 5.3). As mentioned in Chapter 4, when thinking about what is important, we often identify humans as the most important. Consequently, when we look at the photograph, we tend to look at the people first: the playworker and the children. Then, we may look at other things such as the dome that the children are sitting on and the clouds if these catch our eye. While people are involved in creating an atmosphere, they are not the only aspects involved. In Chapter 4, the philosophical approach of posthumanism was introduced as a way to help us consider the different aspects involved in co-creating an atmosphere because it views all things as equally important, not just the humans. When looking at the photograph, such things as the trees, the dome, the bunting, the clouds, the playworker and the children are all equally important. If we were at the playground, rather than just looking at the photograph, we would be able to identify other sensory aspects such as sounds: the wind whistling through the trees, children's laughter and shouts across the playground; smells, such as the smell of freshly mowed grass or smoke from the fire pit; and touch, feeling the change in temperature when the weather changes and raindrops starting to fall. These aspects are what Lorimer (2005:81) refers to as 'more than human', not more in the sense of better but more as in other things. The playful atmosphere is co-created by all these multi-sensory aspects.

The importance of things is not a new idea within playwork as the ideas of affordances and loose parts are often referred to in playwork literature. Gibson (1986), the originator of the term 'affordances', referred to them as possibilities or opportunities offered by the environment – what environmental things offer or afford to people, which also depends on how they are perceived by that individual. For example, a sloping grassy bank offers the opportunity for rolling down, but it is not so good for playing football on. However, not everyone who looks at the grassy bank will view it as an opportunity for rolling down; it may trigger a different response for them. They may want to make use of it in different ways, they may just

Figure 5.3 Monster game. 2022. Courtesy of Truman.

want to sit and relax on it and chat with friends or ride up and down the slope on their bike. How the affordance is used may also be affected by what is allowed or permitted to happen in that space. There may be signs stating 'Keep off the grass' or 'No ball games' and there may be adults around to enforce these rules or express their opinions on what should or should not be happening. However, despite or maybe because of these adult directives, children will still playfully make use of the environment in different ways to those intended by adults. Loose parts are also things that offer and open up possibilities for different ways of interacting with them. Different from an affordance, such as a sloping grassy bank which is an environmental feature, these are things that can be manipulated and/or moved around, such as boxes, sticks, pots, stones, tyres, furniture, material, ropes. Sometimes what children decide is moveable is different from what adults think is moveable. For example, several children at Pitsmoor Adventure Playground were seen moving a long plastic slide from where it was attached to a wooden hut to the other side of the playground to create a different kind of slide experience. Play will find a way.

Deleuze and Guattari (1987) refer to this mixture of different aspects as an assemblage, a collection of things. When we think of a collection of things, we might think of things like an exhibition in a museum and them being quite static and not really changing. However, the assemblage or collection of multi-sensory aspects that co-creates an atmosphere is not fixed, it is a gathering which is constantly changing. Perhaps, as Burnett and Merchant (2016:223) suggest, describing it using the verb 'assembling' would be more helpful. The different aspects assembling in Figure 5.3 will change, for example, it may suddenly grow dark and start to rain or a different child may join the game. These changes occur through interactions between different aspects such as rain falling causing children to move indoors to get out of the rain. We view these as two separate things, the rain and the children, and the effect they have on each other. However, as mentioned in Chapter 4, the posthumanist approach encourages thinking about things as being more than a sum of their individual separate parts, emphasizing their entanglements and connectedness rather than their separateness. To highlight this, rather than using the term 'interaction' which refers to the connections between separate things, the term 'intra-action' (Barad 2007:184) is used. The word 'intra' refers to 'within' or 'inside' one group. For example, we may use the *intra*net at work, the computer network within one organization which is different from the *inter*net, a global computer network, formed between different interconnected networks.

It is this process of intra-action, the combination and entanglement of physical things, people, play equipment, sounds, smells, thoughts and feelings that creates what Lester (2018:85) refers to as 'playspacetimes'. As demonstrated throughout this chapter, playspacetimes can be co-created in diverse spaces, at varied times, and they are not restricted to only occurring in spaces *for* children. For example, the playspacetime referred to by Julia generated in the supermarket was co-created by multiple different aspects in that moment. It did not exist before its co-creation, and when the child left, that playspacetime no longer existed (Lester 2018). It was a one-off, a singular event, and even if this was a game the child regularly played, that particular moment in playspacetime would not happen again the same way. Future games might be similar, might develop from that particular playspacetime, and have traces of it within them (Lester and Russell 2014) but they would be different playspacetimes.

As humans, we are part of the entangled aspects that co-create a playful atmosphere, and as the examples in this chapter have shown, adults' actions and attitudes can affect children's spaces *for* and *of* play. If we are involved in creating the conditions for children's play, this places a 'response-ability' (Lester and Russell 2014:253) on us to be aware of, attuned to and responsive to all the entangled aspects, human and more than human. By being more aware of all these entangled aspects, we can think more broadly, not just focusing on the human element of space and be more aware of the effect of things that might otherwise be taken for granted or overlooked.

6

Age, Risk and Resilience

Chapter Outline

Risk in play and its importance for developing resilience

Lady Allen of Hurtwood – a true champion of children's play – stated, 'Life demands courage, endurance and strength, but we continue to underestimate the capacity of children for taking risks, enjoying the stimulation of danger and finding things out for themselves' (1968:17).

Risk-taking is a topic sure to attract debate and controversy at conferences around the world for the children and young people's workforce. Meanings can vary across sectors and contexts, so using the UK Health and Safety Executive as our source, we clarify these below, as in our experience people often get risks and hazards and our role in responding to each of these confused.

A hazard is anything that may cause harm. Some hazards can be removed or minimized, such as a trailing lead, a slippery floor or broken glass, and we have a responsibility to check for these and do what we can to eliminate or minimize them. Some hazards permanently exist, like traffic or deep water, and we have to find ways to coexist with them or avoid them if necessary.

A risk is the chance that somebody could be harmed, together with an indication of how serious the harm could be. We have a responsibility to assess that possibility and what might happen. In other words, if a risk is taken, something may or may not happen that may or may not have unwanted losses or consequences.

These definitions, however, are constructed in the context of health and safety legislation for employers (in this case, the Health and Safety at Work Act 1974 and the Management of Health & Safety at Work Regulations 1999) as opposed to risk-taking in the context of ordinary life and people's (including children's) behaviour. If we are employed to work with children, then such legislation does apply to our practice. But what the above definitions do not show is the idea that risk-taking in playing may also have 'good' consequences; Gill describes it thus: 'good risks engage and challenge children, and support their growth, learning and development' (2018:9). In this chapter, therefore, we are looking at risk in the context of playing, how and why children seek out opportunities for risky or adventurous play and how we can still support this without contravening health and safety legislation.

Adults and children do perceive risk differently. Having co-managed an adventure playground for several years and delivered playwork training for decades, Ali has had countless conversations with adults about risk-taking when playing – parents and grandparents, foster parents, social workers, psychologists, youth workers, insurance brokers, funders, teachers and head teachers – and the vast majority are initially far more risk-averse than children themselves. While attitudes to play and safety do vary across the world in different social and cultural contexts (Gill 2018), the 'reconfiguration of the risk agenda, in which risk of accidental harm began to dominate peoples' concerns' (Ball-King 2021:1) has generally made risk-aversion become more 'normal' in recent decades (Furedi 2006; Gill 2007; Frost 2010; Lester 2020) with adults being ever more fearful about children's safety (Brussoni et al. 2012; Eager and Little 2011; Guldberg 2009).

In hindsight, it is easy to see how an increase in litigation and health and safety legislation, the professionalization of accident prevention, rising insurance premiums, the media's appetite for tragic stories together with the growth of intrusive social media, have all contributed in recent decades to the view that the world is less safe and has consequently ushered in a ruling paradigm of children's helplessness and need for protection.

It is a popular myth that children have no fear and that this only comes with age. Having seen hundreds of children over the years standing on the edge of playground platforms trying to pluck up the courage to swing or jump off, it is quite clear that they absolutely are fearful of both hurting themselves physically and of emotionally losing face, but they also have a desire to often move past that, to experience the thrills of achievement. One of the big self-built swings at Meriden Adventure Playground was nicknamed the 'Nutter's Platform' by the children themselves, because (and we quote), 'you have to be a nutter to go off that!' To this day, only 50–60 per cent of children attending in any given year do eventually go off it and many climb up there several times and come back down without swinging because they still judge it to be too much of a risk. But for those who finally do jump, the blood-curdling screams of both exhilaration and terror are followed by shrieks of joyful achievement (the following quotes were taken from playworkers' notebooks in the few weeks after the 'Nutters' was first erected).

'That was sick, man!'
'I thought I was going to die!'
'I did it, I did it, I actually did it!'
'Oh, wow, wow, wow, wowzers!'
'That was just incredible!'
'I've got to do it again now – did you see me?!'

Barclay and Tawil (2022a) describe such an experience thus: 'The motivation is the thrill associated with the momentary sense of disequilibrium. . . . Children experience first-hand the feelings associated with mild stress and uncertainty, but within the relative safety of play where risks are relatively low.'

Sandseter (2007) observed six categories of risky experiences that three to five-year-old Norwegian children identified as both scary and fun and seemed to seek out in their play; namely,

- climbing to great heights;
- swinging, skating, riding and sliding at high speed;
- using dangerous tools;
- playing near dangerous elements like fire and deep water;
- rough and tumble – chasing, fighting and wrestling;
- play involving getting lost or 'disappearing'.

Older children, too, regularly seek out such experiences with the contexts getting ever riskier with age and/or size. Most adventure playgrounds of course routinely offer such experiences – hence their popularity with children of all ages, but there are fewer places now where such experiences can be accessed.

In his taxonomy of play types, Hughes lists 'deep play' – play that 'enables children to access risky and even potentially life-threatening experiences' (2002:12). We agree with Hughes that the intention is to risk possible death and survive, not to actually die (ibid:13) and that this has both a developmental and an evolutionary purpose. Sandseter too, went on to propose that risky play experiences have an anti-phobic function, enabling children to cope with fear (Sandseter and Kennair 2011).

Adults forget that many of us also from time to time engage in deep play; by drinking to excess, taking drugs, driving at speed, gambling, taking part in challenging activities or extreme sports, climbing mountains, wild swimming and so on. The perception and experience of deep play is very much an individual thing whether adult or child; what is deep play to one human being may not be at all to another. We have seen a barefooted five-year-old scampering sure-footedly up a high pyramid climbing frame and balancing on the top without a care in the world (even though we all had our hearts in our mouths at the time!) and a few minutes later watched a ten-year-old climbing shakily up three rungs onto a ledge with terrified determination. The ten-year-old was accessing deep play, not the five-year-old.

As adults around children playing, we need to find ways to support deep play and other forms of playful risk-taking. Repressing or banning these kinds of play actually denies children's ability to make and trust their own judgements and build their own competencies, and if we do so, we can cause them to ultimately be more afraid and dependent and less safe in the world. Refusing children these experiences on the shifting grounds that we feel better or won't get sued is not a solution (Gill 2018; Dodd and Lester 2021; Ball, Gill and Spiegel 2012; Grey 2014). What are your views on this?

Even in possibly the most risk-averse setting of all – a prison – playworkers have found ways to support children visiting incarcerated relatives. Emma tells us that the resources that playworkers in prison are allowed to have are severely limited as they are seen as too much of a risk if they got into prisoners' hands. Balloons, pipe-cleaners, red paint, tents and tunnels, games with batteries, playdough, scissors, elastic bands, toy guns, large cardboard boxes, masks, string, rope, foil, cornflour, cotton wool and wax crayons are all on the not-allowed list in English prisons as these could be misused or create weapons. Pencils, paintbrushes and glue sticks have to be individually counted in and out of play sessions to prevent the prison going into lockdown. Playworkers, therefore, have to be very flexible and adaptable in their approach to overcome the restrictions and still create a space to play. For visiting children, the experience can be traumatizing in itself, and playworkers take great care in supporting children to play while there and to play out how they feel. Despite the constraining precautions that inhibit so much physical risk-taking, there is often real emotional risk-taking by children during these sessions. Emma told us that sometimes while waiting for prisoners to be brought by prison officers into the visiting hall, children were running and leaping over the chairs while they still could, and playworkers of course did not deter them. Where there's a will, there's a way to help children play and thrive.

Risk has become both a characteristic and an inevitable consequence of modernity, say Muller-Mahn, Everts and Stephan (2018:3). A recent conversation with a retired UK youth and community worker, now in his late seventies, who had managed a large statutory staff team up until 1990, illustrated this saying that during the 1960s through to the mid-1980s, none of his staff were required to have health and safety policies or risk assessments because accidents rarely happened and 'we all used our common sense'. Practice has changed so radically in the UK in just three decades, and we are having conversations with adults that would never have been necessary back then.

Nevertheless, the playwork sector in the UK has worked tirelessly in this time to address this increasing focus on risk and the main 'weapon' in their armoury has been risk-benefit assessments. Ball-King (2021:3) recognized the contributions of the UK Play Safety Forum in highlighting the need to balance or 'trade-off' both risks and benefits if children – and adults – were to experience the health and well-being gains of play, leisure and recreation. In playwork, we call it risk-benefit assessment (RBA) whereas he refers to benefit-risk assessment (B-RA), but it is essentially the same process. He goes on to chart how understanding and application of assessment of both benefits and risks have been slowly gaining ground in the leisure industry and more recently in healthcare and aviation, and he believes that the concept is now very common outside playwork, but not often recognized for what it is. So how do we undertake such an assessment of what we see children doing?

As expected, we need to identify possible risks and what the consequences of these might be. But we also need to identify the benefits of taking such risks – what can be gained physically, socially and emotionally from this activity? It sounds relatively simple, but to be as accurate and as practical as possible takes thought and care – this kind of assessment is not a scientific measurement with definite right and wrong answers because it involves individuals of different ages, capability and experience with a likely range of needs and opinions in an ever-changing space with a variety of possible props.

If we take climbing trees as an example, we would first need to identify which trees are being climbed (not all of them are safe to climb!) and then we could perhaps safely say that the risks might include getting scratched by bark or twigs, getting trapped and unable to go up or down, and then slipping and/or falling, which could result in bruising, cuts, sprains, fractures or concussion. There may be other considerations depending on the tree and where it is sited, the height and strength of the lower and upper branches, whether there are any nests (birds, wasps, bees, etc.) and so on. Just assessing the risks could easily convince some people that it is too dangerous an activity!

But then we start to list the potential benefits of climbing trees, which might include

- a sense of achievement;
- confidence building;
- increased stamina and muscle growth;
- improved balance;
- improved eye/hand/foot co-ordination;
- conquering fear;
- cardiovascular exercise;
- problem-solving – a route up and down;
- improving attempts, not giving up;
- learning to manage/cope with risk;
- exhilaration of being high up or off the ground;
- experiencing a close-up encounter with nature;
- excitement, fun (Figure 6.1).

Then we begin to ask ourselves why would we not support or allow tree-climbing! And then we begin to think of what else we could do to make tree climbing possible for as many children as possible. We might, for instance,

Figure 6.1 Easy when you know how. 2023. Courtesy of King.

- decide to observe closely (but as unobtrusively as possible) to get an idea of children's competencies or abilities;
- discuss with particular children (if needed) where feet and/or hands can sensibly/realistically go;
- build confidence by verbally recognizing their achievements;
- talk with children about limiting numbers (if needed);
- encourage children to take responsibility for themselves and each other;
- recognize that some children are very able and agile, and what is risky for one child is not the same for every child.

We might not do some of the above, but certainly we do need to observe because that is how we learn (a) about what children are capable of rather than making assumptions and (b) whether anything else might be needed from us. Adults sometimes think that safety mats at the bottom of the tree or blocks to climb up from would help, but sometimes these 'aids' can actually hinder rather than help and give an illusion of safety that doesn't necessarily enable children to develop their own ideas and skills.

We might also want to consider

- local factors, for example, *who else might be watching or likely to intervene, whether the health and safety policy is supportive of the activity, what children are wearing;*
- precedents and/or comparisons, for example, *has this been tried or done before, has this been done elsewhere, what experience do children have or not have of this;*
- decisions made, for example, *particular trees were regarded as insufficiently safe or suitable for climbing, activity not undertaken due to inclement weather, children attaching ropes to lower branches need further assessment of both risks and benefits after introducing these;*
- actions taken, for example, *closer observation, undertaking further inspection of particular trees, identifying further resources (e.g. ropes or lengths of fabric) to increase challenge and creativity (e.g. making swings or ladders).*

Besides making written records of RBAs, we need to be undertaking dynamic RBA, where we are literally going through the process in our heads as playing evolves in front of us and children do something unexpected or different from what has gone on before. Playworkers will often say they are constantly practising dynamic RBA and making decisions about what children are doing.

Recording RBAs before and after play is a useful practice as it provides evidence of reflection, decisions and actions taken. Such evidence can be needed to assure and convince insurers, managers, teachers or parents, and can be used as a reflective and/or training tool with staff and volunteers. Ali recalls undertaking a project to promote lunchtime play in a primary school where the head teacher was so risk-averse that children were not even allowed to run in the playground in case they fell over and hurt themselves. The only sounds to be heard in the playground were children moaning and arguing, and lunchtime staff were constantly dealing with complaints of boredom and aggression. Explaining the RBA process to the head teacher and encouraging him to come outside each lunchtime and watch what was happening and how children were playing made an enormous difference. This head teacher had simply never thought through his previous decisions and their consequences, but bravely took the time to rethink and look at the evidence in front of him, and within three months the children were climbing trees, building rope swings and dens, and there was laughter and shouting with busy, active children. Properly assessing the benefits as well as the risks opens up a whole new playful world.

Recorded RBAs need regular reviewing and updating as different children do things differently and can often surprise us! Monitoring children's risk-taking when playing is messy and complex in reality and, as Ball-King (2021) argues, should be descriptive and not quantitative in form, recognizing the contributory expertise of practitioners in making personal judgements based on clear practice-based values and understandings. We agree, although we do know playworkers who try to also include some quantitative information in the form of 'scoring' the risk level because they say that seems to communicate more easily with insurance brokers and those teachers who, in practice, tend to be more risk-averse. We include an example in Appendix 3, taken from a playwork project in a primary school where children were play fighting – something they love to do that many schools disallow, but this school was persuaded by regular RBA that this was risky play, not fighting.

Despite the fact that fixed play areas and theme parks often have age limits on certain pieces of equipment or rides, age is often inappropriate or even irrelevant in terms of children's risk-taking abilities. Obviously, as their cognitive development progresses and they physically grow bigger, this makes a difference in their capabilities and competencies, but their feelings, previous experiences, any additional needs they have plus the reactions of caregivers and other adults are all relevant factors too. Using a child's age to decide what they can or cannot do may seem like a simple solution for adults trying to protect them, but it also removes all sense of responsibility from the child too, which can ultimately make them less safe.

The 'visible cliff' experiment undertaken in the 1960s (Gibson and Walk 1960) was done at the time to investigate whether depth perception was innate, but for our purposes, it is interesting to note that despite maternal encouragement, the large majority of crawling babies refused to cross the glass when they could see the 'drop'. Even young babies have an instinct to keep themselves safe – something we should be working alongside them to encourage, rather than taking all the responsibility ourselves. Recent research with children aged seventeen to twenty-five months similarly shows that toddlers are quite able to assess and manage risks in challenging natural environments and do develop their own risk management skills (Sandseter 2022).

Another controversial subject around children and risk-taking is that of digital play (we also make a brief reference to this in Chapter 8). The debate has been heated and is still ongoing, with many parents feeling they should limit on-screen time to reduce the possibility of addiction and access to certain games. We are minded that such debates are not new – when comics and then television first became available, there was a similar sense of moral panic because these were unfamiliar and outside of parent's own experience.

Frost (2010) lists cyber-play as one of the ingredients of the 'perfect storm' of play deprivation and laments its effects on the brains and bodies of children left to play on electronic devices with little adult control over time and content. Singer and Singer (2005), however, suggest that while over-exposure to electronic media violence is undoubtedly toxic, electronic media can make a positive contribution to imagination, empathy and creativity. While a number of studies have claimed that regular video gaming has resulted in violence, aggression and poor mental health, more recent research is finding increased performance on cognitive skills tests involving impulse control and working memory (Chaarani et al. 2022).

As always, there is a balance to be found, and the pros and cons of regular digital play will not be simply charted. The reality is that most children and young people are regularly playing games on a range of devices, and that is not likely to change. That does mean that some children may be spending too much time (but how much is too much?) on this and may suffer associated harmful effects like addiction, obesity and/or aggression. It does not mean that most children are therefore never accessing play in other contexts or going outdoors, or that virtual and non-virtual play are separate from each other – 'traditional play and technology are interwoven; hybrid' (Martin 2017a:2).

Marsh et al. purport that contemporary digital cultures provide rich 'converged' opportunities for playing in new imaginative ways: 'contemporary play draws on both the digital and non-digital properties of things and in doing so, moves fluidly across boundaries of space and time in ways that were not possible in the pre-digital era' (2016:247). Martin describes an adventure playground as 'a hybrid environment of the organic, material and socio-cultural, located not only in geographical space but also in cyberspace, where diverse actants converge, assemble and diverge in ever changing assemblages' (2017b:170). As with all forms of playing, digital play will have its risks as well as its benefits and we would do well to pay attention to both, recognizing that it is an important part of many children's lives. Fisher (2023) reminds us that many children's experience of digital play is about making connections, regulating emotions, being creative, feeling alive, solving problems, resolving conflicts, as well as being a valuable learning tool. She warns us that fear of screens and addiction can be so ingrained in adults that they are unable to see that gaming is a relief and a solution rather than a problem for many children.

There has been a societal tendency to associate risk with physical actions and consequences, but a huge component of children's risk-taking involves emotions. Uncertainty, daring, loss of face, hurt pride, engaging with the unknown, exposing one's true self, ideas, humour, capabilities – these are all emotional risks (Barclay and Tawil 2022b). Understanding this makes sense of how playing can build resilience – overcoming fear and uncertainty and discovering that one can survive such experiences builds confidence and a willingness to re-engage.

Resilience (also referred to in Chapter 7) has become rather a buzzword in recent years, and there have been a number of definitions in circulation with different waves of research (Roisman et al. 2002; Masten 2007, 2011; Ungar 2008, 2012, 2015). These definitions vary according to both internal and external perspectives and interventions, that is, the psychological make-up of the individual that enables them to cope or 'bounce back', the nature of adversity an individual may be facing (and whether that is cultural or structural), and the interventions that could be made to either support an individual and/or change the situation. We like Hart et al.'s definition – 'beating the odds whilst also changing the odds' as their holistic approach considers the individual child, the impact of both structural and societal inequalities upon the child and those responsible for her or him, while also proposing 'resilient moves – small changes that could be made quickly and which acknowledge where the young person is starting from' (2016:1).

If resilience is about an ability to cope with the unexpected and to bounce back from adversity, then it is clearly key to emotional and physical health and well-being. Lester and Russell (2008:50) say that when playing, children consciously and unconsciously express and refine common adaptive systems which include:

- emotion regulation;
- pleasure and enjoyment, and the promotion of positive feelings;
- stress response systems and the ability to create and respond to uncertainty;
- creativity and the ability to make novel connections;
- learning;
- attachment to people and places.

These systems (explored more in Chapter 7) can easily be observed occurring naturally during play and make a significant contribution to equipping children to manage and survive the challenges in their ongoing lives. The evidence in Lester and Russell's research review shows that essentially play is indeed 'ordinary magic' and an important factor in building resilience. If we return to the example given earlier of children going off the Nutter's platform at Meriden Adventure Playground, we can immediately see how the above systems are naturally employed, as they are with other such activities there.

Adventure playgrounds and out-of-school clubs have in recent years had to work hard to justify not just the importance of play for all-round child development but also the importance of children's freedom and independence, which includes their ability to assess and take risks for themselves. We would argue that places to play genuinely and freely, where there are caring and supportive adults around, are important resources/environments that will naturally foster increased resilience.

Aumann and Hart very practically propose that resilience is more about 'things that happen, or resources that we might put in place, that improve the odds for a child where they are stacked against them' (2009:10). Children do have to cope with life and what it throws at them, but in order to do this, they also need a supportive physical and emotional environment, which can be manifested in many different ways. Aumann and Hart (2009: 48) visualize a 'magic box' full of spells and potions – essentially a toolkit – that depict all the possible resources and interventions necessary for supporting and strengthening a child. The majority of these are applicable to good playwork provision, for example:

1. the **basics** of exercise and fresh air, playtime and leisure, feeling safe;
2. supporting children to **cope**, be brave, solve problems, foster their interests, self-soothe;
3. enabling children to **belong**, feel part of things, make and keep relationships and friendships;
4. helping children to **learn**, develop life skills, organize themselves and highlight achievements;
5. building their '**core self**' by instilling hope, helping them understand their own and other's perspectives and feelings, fostering their talents and independence.

Playwork provision that supports free playful expression, understands the need for risk-taking in play, and builds caring, supportive and power-sharing relationships with children also enables children to build greater resilience.

Meriden Adventure Playground shared with us the results of their ongoing evaluations and reflections, where children and young people have described the playground as their 'happy place', their 'safe space', their 'sanctuary', 'the place where I can really be me', 'somewhere I know I will be listened to', 'where I feel free'. Parents and carers also stated that the playground is 'a god-send', 'the best place for kids', 'X's go-to place for letting off steam', 'a confidence-builder' and testify to how much their children have developed and grown and 'cope so much better with things'. Playworkers there have noticed that since Covid, children have engaged far more with sensory resources like large trays or buckets of slime, or paint and cornflour – often immersing themselves in this with eyes closed and bare hands, making rhythmical movements over and over. Children and their parents have often spontaneously commented how calming this is and how they 'feel better' and 'cope more'. One of the playworkers discovered videos of art therapy for traumatized adults doing exactly the same thing with thick paint or chalk. It was not lost on the playground staff that given permission and materials, children seemed to instinctively know what to do to help themselves express and release particular emotions, or as Russell, Barclay and Tawil propose 'when conditions are right, children can create their own well-being' (2023: 9).

'Play safety is complex territory. But children's health and well-being should be at the centre and not too focussed on risk reduction at the expense of children's engagement, enjoyment and learning' (Gill 2018:32). Adventurous play, including deep play, where children have opportunities to be in control of experiencing fear, thrill, uncertainty and excitement, also enable them to overcome anxiety, regulate their feelings and increase their capacity to survive. It is our individual and collective responsibility to understand that such opportunities are needed and to ensure that all children can access these.

7
Emotions and Resilience

Chapter Outline

Emotional engagement and experience when playing

When we – children or adults – play, it is absolutely as much (if not more) about how we feel as it is about what we do, although that is not commonly expressed in many books and articles about play. Much more tends to be said about the actions of playing rather than the experience itself. But in truth,

> When we watch a child play, we only see a small part of what is going on. Children play with their whole selves: it is a somatic, sensual, emotional, cognitive, social and spiritual phenomenon. All we see is the external manifestation. (Russell 2005:104)

When we recall our own play memories, it is often with a re-experience of how we felt at the time – we have witnessed this many times on courses and seminars where we have asked adults to remember how they played, and the room slowly fills with animated excitement and laughter. When we ask them how they felt in their memories, they are always very vocal and give rich examples right across the emotional spectrum, including frustration, fear, anger, joy, sadness, wonder and so on.

We also regularly observe the emotional content of children's play in the present. We see them (a) experimenting with feelings in their games, (b) exploring how they feel and (c) fully expressing the emotions they are experiencing – as the following recent examples show.

   a) A group of boys aged eight to twelve years were taking it in turns to be a dogmatic and autocratic leader, with all the others submitting to whatever the leader asked of them – which tended to be simple tasks like 'bring me this' or 'do that for me'. When the task got too outrageous or unpleasant – as it always expectedly did – (e.g. 'lie down in front of me with your face in the mud') the group finally revolted and there was a change of leader. There was an air of hilarity about the game during each 'coup', but also a definite sense of trying out what it felt like to both wield power and to be temporarily powerless and there was an almost palpable sense of relief when they could vote out each leader and start again.

b) A group of several boys and girls aged six to ten years attending a local playscheme discovered a dead mouse outside and then spent the rest of that day having three different funerals and burials – one was Catholic, one was evangelical and one was Moslem. They all took roles of either wailers and mourners (who really sobbed), priest or preacher (who gave stirring speeches which invoked more crying) and they made and inscribed a wooden headstone (having named the mouse and given it a whole life history). One child was later heard to say 'it's really fun to be sad sometimes'.

c) At an adventure playground where a new deep crash mat had been donated, children wanted it laid next to one of the platforms so they could jump onto it. In the weeks that followed, children of all ages queued up to try this and to perfect their moves. To begin with, a significant number scaled the ladder onto the platform, looked down and then climbed

Figure 7.1 Will I make it? 2022. Courtesy of Keeling.

back down saying it was far too scary. But slowly over time, with lots of deliberation and observation of others, the majority got to conquering their fear and taking what clearly felt like (and was!) a huge risk and jumping off, which in time for many turned into somersaulting off both forwards and backwards. The sounds, screams, shouts and whoops that followed were amazing – the heady combination of absolute fear, (oh my god, I'm going to kill myself . . .) the thrill of the 'flight' (this is just sooo awesome) and the confidence boost (I did it, I did it!) didn't stop being talked about for weeks and it was great to see children later applauding others on their first jump! (Figure 7.1).

Sturrock postulated that 'the playing out of affective material (is) one of the prime functions of play' (2002:4). The examples above and the many many more that we regularly see certainly show that children are fully engaging emotionally in their playing. Is this just an expected and natural component of playing, or does it – as Sturrock intimates – indicate an evolved and necessary function?

Looking up the word 'feelings' in any thesaurus gives us a wide spectrum of possibilities from intuition to a concrete perspective, appreciation to passion, bodily sensation to touch, passing sentiment to a presiding mood, attitude to belief. 'Feeling' can be described in physical, mental or spiritual terms; it can be internal or external and it can be ascribed to an individual or even, it seems a whole nation. Little wonder that Claparede said that 'the psychology of the affective processes is the most confused chapter in all psychology' (1928:157).

The last few decades, however, have seen a big increase in studies of emotions, their origin, their purpose, their experience, their consequences and their management. This has been welcome as prior to this, emotions were still somewhat regarded with suspicion and 'this culturally transmitted fear of emotions' (Orbach 1994:6) taught most of us that suppression was the order of the day and that emotions were only considered if they became 'a problem', meaning that 'less was known about the emotional development of normal children, than of deprived, disturbed or delinquent children' (Pringle 1986:21). Research has resulted in thousands of self-help and therapy books and a plethora of counselling opportunities, as people wrestle with their own emotional lives. But it is advances in neuroscience that have really put this topic on the map. 'As the field began to better understand emotional circuitry in the brain, emotion became "observable" in a sense and thus was viewed as a legitimate focus for science' (Southam-Gerow 2013:4). There are now clearer aspects of how we develop emotionally throughout childhood and beyond and therefore how such development might be helped or hindered.

So what constitutes normative positive emotional development? We use the word 'normative' here because 'theories of child development which articulate ages and stages at which it is believed certain behaviours are appropriate/normal/necessary for psychological and physical well-being and maturation . . . tend to assume a universal child who is without gender, class or ethnicity' (Gittins 1998:15).

Generally, however, there is agreement that normative emotional development encompasses:

1. Developing a wide-ranging emotional capacity. This begins with the experience of primary emotions such as anger, fear and pleasure as an infant, which evolve into further differentiated forms with the onset of memory and a variety of new experiences and new capabilities. Sroufe states that such emotional evolution is 'experience dependent' (1997:25), although quite what experiences are necessary and how often they should occur is somewhat debatable, but we would argue that an ever-increasing range of play experiences would be essential.
2. The ability to both cognitively and physically identify and recognize different emotions in both one's self and in others (Leigh 2017). This gives rise to the growth of empathy and being able to understand different perspectives.
3. The ability to accept and manage one's own and others' emotions and to respond appropriately – this has also been termed as having emotional intelligence (Goleman 1996) or becoming emotionally literate.

Two particular areas of the brain are involved, and as we grow and have different experiences, the emotional circuitry between these areas – the amygdala at the back of the brain and the pre-frontal cortex at the front – increases. The amygdala – sometimes called the limbic or reptilian brain because it exists in reptiles – is that part of the brain fuelled by adrenaline that facilitates conditioned responses and reflexes such as fight or flight. When we are startled or suddenly come under pressure; when we feel a flood of those often irrational primary emotions (Darwin 1872, Damasio 1999) such as anger, surprise, disgust, fear, sadness and happiness, these are prompted by the amygdala. If we immediately act on these without thought, we could sometimes regret it later as not being the wisest course of action. When mammals evolved, however, their brains had an additional frontal cortex – this is the part of the brain that pays attention to our first reactions and considers what to do, rather than therefore just reacting impulsively or instinctively. This gives rise to the more rational secondary emotions (Damasio 2003) such as pride, envy, shame, guilt and embarrassment that moderate the unruly primary emotions and therefore our consequent behaviour. This 'thinking' part of the brain increases in capacity and capability throughout mammalian evolution into humankind. Clearly, having both of these parts of the brain working together increases the chance of survival.

Sutton-Smith (2017), perhaps the most famous play theorist, believed that play was the primary mechanism for increasing and improving this neural development. He suggests that play may have begun with the emergence of mammalian life and therefore serves a serious survival function. Certainly mammalian animals do play and do display emotion, as shown by researchers like Panksepp (2000), Burghardt (2005) and Bekoff (2007). Sutton-Smith's contention is that 'perturbing basic emotions have to be kept under control in real life and that is why the struggles they create become represented in our play' (2017:81). In other words, play is the stage upon which we rehearse our battles, test our prowess, explore reactions and responses, flirt with danger, experience and express strong feelings, try out situations, roles and strategies, feel in charge and gain mastery and make sense of the world around us. Playing allows us to access and experiment with our more vigorous emotions and feel alive, while simultaneously overcoming and controlling those feelings rather than being at their mercy. As Sutton-Smith says,

> Play was always intended to serve a healing function whether for child or adult, making it more worthwhile to defy the depressing and dangerous aspects of life. Play is neurologically a reactive itch of the amygdala, one that responds to archetypal shock, anger, fear, disgust and sadness. But play also includes a frontal-lobe counter, reaching for triumphant control and happiness and pride. (2017:60)

Is this 'duality' of emotion in play why we so regularly see children playfighting and staging mock battles; imagining different worlds where they are finally superheroes saving the day and good eventually wins over evil; playing a wide range of real and imagined roles and characters; immersed in reflection, negotiation and exploration; exhibiting often exhausted but deep satisfaction at the end of playing? Is this why playing children shout and scream, laugh and cry, engage in teasing and banter, test friends as well as foes, make furious demands and build or find secret places where they can hide or think? We cannot presently be certain, but in his final book, Sutton-Smith (2017) makes a powerful argument that playworkers and others working with children the world over would recognize.

This prompts us to consider the obvious connection here to resilience. We tend to think of resilience as the ability to bounce back from stress rather than be overwhelmed by it. But how we do that, whether we can always do that and what helps or hinders us doing it, has been the subject of much multi-disciplinary research recently, some of which we refer to in Chapter 6. Definitions of resilience have ranged widely depending on whether they are focused on the individual, a community, a culture or the environment. Like emotion, and like play, this is another complex moving target which defies simple categorization. Much research has taken place around the individual, family, community and societal factors associated with resilience and what therefore may support or obstruct its development. But although this is useful, many studies do not specifically address how children naturally develop resilience in their playing. Sutton-Smith laments 'what seems to me to be truly remarkable is that serious, scientific, child psychology has largely ignored the vast amount of real-life emotional data on childhood, which clearly displays the rough-and-tumble emotional life of children' (2017:135).

Lester and Russell (2008) did a sterling job in their examination of a range of research studies, which drew out significant findings of how play can foster resilience in children, although it must be stressed here that this does not mean that it is adults who can therefore use play activities to 'train' children into being more resilient. We are talking here about children and young people themselves 'determining and controlling the content and intent of their play, by following their own instincts, ideas and interests, in their own way for their own reasons' (PPSG 2005) – a very different scenario. It is such playing that 'deals with the borderline between being in control and being out of control, but in play being in control is the frame within which you may safely be out of control' (Miller 1974:46). The boy who took some old keyboards (that were available for play) behind the bushes in a school playground and smashed them up and then came out saying 'that's the best anger management I've ever had' knew what we are saying here.

The following story is another good example.

Tyler – aged eleven – usually came weekly to an adventure playground with a group from the Pupil Referral Unit he attended (all of whom had been excluded from school due to their aggressive behaviour), but turned up on his own one weekend during a public session – this was the first time he had done this.

A playworker (Simon) greeted him warmly as he arrived, noting that he seemed angry and upset and when Tyler went and sat heavily on a wooden base, Simon sat by him and asked if he was okay. Tyler replied 'It's not fair – it's always me that gets the trouble. I wouldn't mind if it was me that did it, but I didn't and I still got in trouble'.

Simon knew Tyler fairly well and was aware of the social dynamics in the PRU group and what often transpired. He suggested to Tyler that because he was bigger and louder than his peers he was more noticed and that if there was trouble brewing and he wasn't part of it, perhaps he could help himself more if he moved away from those causing hassle. This was talked about for a little while.

Tyler then asked for a hammer and nails and Simon got him some – this was often a way children 'got their anger out' by banging nails into pieces of wood. He then went to the woodpile and carefully chose an old bannister spindle and started strategically knocking nails into one end. Simon stayed close by pretending to sort the woodpile but actually keeping a close eye on Tyler, as if he lost his temper, Simon knew this could endanger others and there were a lot of other children on site.

After a short time, Simon stood and watched Tyler and then commented that his 'creation' looked a lot like a weapon. 'Yes it is', he said forcefully. Simon continued to watch and said casually that actually it looked a lot like a mace which is a ceremonial weapon carried by a bishop who is not allowed to carry a blade or a sword. Tyler asked a couple of questions while Simon weaved a story about a mace representing authority and peace rather than violence and how it is still used today in various countries' parliaments. Tyler seemed to take this in and after a lull in conversation; he then stood up and put his hands underneath his 'weapon' lifting it up so that it lay flat across his palms.

He then proceeded to walk slowly and purposefully towards the firepit where a fire was burning. Simon walked slowly with him, wondering what Tyler was going to do and planning to put himself between Tyler and any others at the firepit if that became necessary. To Simon's amazement, Tyler walked over to the fire and with great ceremony and seemingly oblivious to the other children around the fire circle who were lighting candles and poking the fire, he walked slowly through them, got down on one knee and solemnly placed the now heavily spiked spindle into the flames as though offering up treasure. He then stepped back, sat up straight on a nearby stump and both he and Simon watched together as it slowly burnt. When it broke apart into embers, so did the spell holding their attention and Tyler – no longer angry - moved away and went off to play elsewhere. (Rix 2016)

Very often this kind of playing is frowned upon by adults who might regard it as unsafe and/or antisocial. Sutton-Smith suggests that adults often 'find themselves 'lost' on children's playgrounds because they do not speak the language of play' (2017:135) – they therefore judge what they see and hear from an adult perspective and hardly ever the child's. But play is the child's domain and the child's world and we adults must recognize that we have ceased to be the experts. In the story told above, Tyler powerfully and meaningfully makes sense of and plays out his deep-seated frustration in his own way, with the sensitive support of the 'transformative relationship' (Ungar 2013) that had been built over time with the playworker. As psychiatrist Shooter says,

'Free play gives the growing child the cognitive ability to solve problems, the emotional ability to withstand hardship, the social ability to help each other, and the physical ability to carry it all through. Play is the foundation stone of resilience in children, no matter what life may throw at them!' (2020:2)

Lester and Russell (2008) bring together evidence that suggests resilience is associated with the operation of the following interrelated adaptive systems:

- Emotion regulation – the unique 'as if' nature of play offers children opportunities to explore a variety of emotional responses. Violence, death, bodily functions, loss and tragedy often feature in pretend play. 'The advantage of playing is that you can test out the actions and emotions that would be too dangerous to act out in real life' (Hendricks 2011:228). This increases flexibility and adaptability – both needed for resilient responses under stress.
- Pleasure and enjoyment and the promotion of positive feelings – play that is under children's control promotes a sense of satisfaction and 'well-being' which drives a desire to carry on exploring and playing. 'Is it any wonder that often the times we feel most alive, those that make up our best memories, are moments of play?' (Brown 2009:5). Playing makes children happier and more resilient.
- Stress response systems – children regularly introduce low-level stresses and anxieties into their games in order to gain mastery over them and to experience feelings of excitement and bravery. Games like 'Chinese burns', 'knuckle raps' and 'slaps' where children are willingly inflicting minor pain on themselves and each other are examples. Most of us remember playing such games, but what is our response now when we see children playing them ('don't hurt each other'? 'play nicely'?). These positive stresses (Rutter 2006) actually help children develop better ways of coping with and adapting to both present and future life events.

- Creativity – in play, children come up with fantastic and often apparently bizarre inventions and ideas, which demonstrates the capacity for problem-solving to support ever-flexible responses. Play is the 'ideal setting or jumping-off point for creative thinking' (Newson and Newson 1979: 12).
- Learning – children do learn masses through playing although that is not necessarily why they play. Because play is fun and under their control, this increases their motivation to more meaningfully explore, experience and discover themselves and their environment. 'Self-directed play experiences nourish and support the child's maturing mental abilities' (Elkind 2007:128).
- Attachment to people and places – a necessary sense of belonging to and with others and to and with particular spaces which may already exist, or that children themselves may create. Play has a key role in helping to develop strong attachments through place-making (Beunderman 2010) and in building self-identity and social capital (Putnam 2000), all of which helps children explore who they are and where they 'fit' in a world that doesn't always accept them as they are or promote their rights.

Self-directed play experiences have a central role in building resilience and in enabling natural emotional development throughout childhood. It stands to reason, therefore, that the more freedom, time and space to play children have, the better this will support their emotional health and well-being and abilities to cope with the ups and downs of their lives. But self-directed play – play where children themselves are in charge – is not as understood or as accepted as we would like. It is still so common that adults feel that they know better and they should control children's play – especially when it exhibits what might be perceived as unsafe or antisocial behaviour. This is perhaps understandable when most of the time we adults do have a legitimate role in educating and protecting children. But what we often fail to realize is that children themselves also have such a role – how will they ever learn to keep themselves safe if they are never away from adult eyes and control? How will they ever discover their powers of critical thinking if they are not allowed to explore and think for themselves? How will they ever take responsibility for themselves and each other if they are not given regular opportunities to do so? We adults still find it hard to believe that children are enormously capable and competent, but the more opportunities they have to be in control of their own playing, the more their skills and confidence grow as seen in the following example.

> Ali worked in an infant school (children aged four to seven years) for a few months installing a Scrapstore Playpod full of loose parts (see www.playpods.co.uk), training lunchtime playground staff and then mentoring them over several weeks in the playground so that they gained confidence in using a playwork approach.
>
> The children were very responsive and began using the loose parts in a variety of ways – building swings, dens, shops, rockets, towers, homes and offices and all the previous playground problems of arguments, conflicts and boredom disappeared almost overnight.
>
> Returning several months later to see how things were going, it was good to see that play was still thriving and the lunchtime staff were still 'playworking', but Ali was most heartened to hear from the headteacher that on their recent annual residential school trip to an outdoor adventure centre, both he and his staff were amazed to find that the children were nothing like as clingy, as scared or as timid as they had been on all previous trips. The children all enthusiastically had a go at all the activities, helped and looked after each other and 'didn't seem to really need us'. The headteacher said he felt this change could only be due to the fact that the children were now so used to daily directing their own play at school, that their confidence and all-round ability had really grown and was substantially higher than that which staff would normally expect.

We would argue that if children are deprived of self-directed play, then they will be more dependent and insecure and less capable and curious. We do need to recognize that if we want to encourage independence and resilience in children, we have to give them freedom and experiences to foster this; chances to make their own mistakes and learn from them; opportunities to test out their own theories and their limits. We need to realize we are not as necessary as we like to think we are; in fact, playing freely with peers has been shown to be fundamental for physical, social and emotional development (Suomi and Harlow 1971, Webb and Brown 2003) and the more we limit children playing together or interfere with it, the more we inhibit such development.

Here is a story from Becky, a foster carer.

> Becky first began to have Andrew on weekend respite care when he was eight years old and this soon became a full-time placement. Andrew had been taken into care at the age of five with a diagnosis of autism and developmental delay and a background of neglect in a larger family with much older siblings.
>
> When Andrew first arrived, Becky reported that he ran up and down a lot (a form of stimming) but didn't touch or play with objects and communicated little. At the time she was also looking after two toddlers aged three who spent a

lot of time playing with dolls. Andrew began to watch this with interest and before long started to copy them and join in at a similar level and express pleasure at doing so.

Becky also had a son Lewis, who was a similar age to Andrew and after several weeks playing with the toddlers, Andrew began to then take interest in watching Lewis playing 'cops and robbers'. Eventually Andrew started to copy and join in with Lewis, making efforts to talk in both goodie and baddie roles. Slowly he began to talk more generally and to make the connections between feelings in role-play and real life.

Becky reports that before then, Andrew would look blank when asked if he was sad or angry, but as he took Lewis's lead and immersed himself in the storyline of 'cops and robbers', he began to understand that it is sad to be in jail, it is scary to be chased by police and so on, and before long Andrew started to both recognize and talk about his real-life emotions and also understand that others have feelings too.

Becky remarked that it was amazing to see how naturally playing with other children and experiencing the power of pretend play and role-play was 'replacing the bricks missing in his social and emotional development. Foster children have often missed out so much on normal developmental play. They just need other – often younger – children, some stuff to play with and a supportive adult in the background who gives permission and shows interest when needed – and then they just make up all that ground'. (conversation 24/04/20)

This echoes Brown's conclusions after a year's research playwork project with traumatized and neglected children in a Romanian hospital, who

showed benefit from the interaction with an infant going through the early stages of development. In less than a year, these chronically abused and neglected children made the sort of progress on the road to recovery, that many experts assumed would be impossible. During the period of the research study the only change in the children's life experience was the playwork project. Therefore, it is sensible to ask what it is about playwork that has contributed to these changes. Apart from some very specific work focusing on each child's personal agenda, the most fundamental causal factor was undoubtedly the fact that these children now had play-mates – that, and the example provided by the White Rose Initiative playworkers who were encouraged to treat the children with love and respect at all times. (Brown 2013:5)

Meares and Keeling (2016:8) put forward a 'socio-ecological' model as a lens through which to better explore resilience, rather than the usual consideration of individual personal qualities or family and social

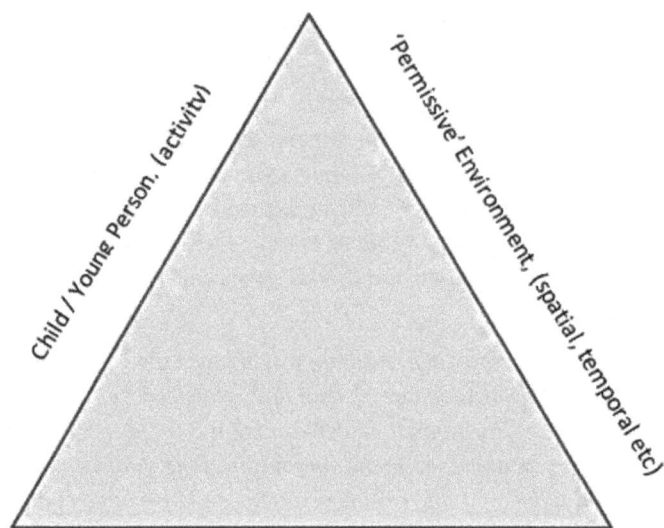

Figure 7.2 Socio-ecological model. 2016. Courtesy of Meares.

factors. This model, Figure 7.2, comprises a triad of interrelated elements, highlighting the fundamental need for free play in the context of (a) a 'permissive' and stimulating environment and (b) a relationship with an adult (or adults) who offer space for questioning and rethinking (as in the mace story given above). The playing is essential, but the back-up of the human/environmental context can also 'recognise, nurture and empower children's (auto) resilience'.

This makes us pause and consider how we adults – parents, caregivers and professionals – are genuinely supporting children's play, in terms of giving time, space, freedom, respect and recognition.

Depriving children of play experiences that are widely regarded as developmentally essential will 'result in those affected being biologically and socially disabled', says Hughes (2003:1) and psychotherapist Fearns (2020:1) – also quoting Gaskill and Perry (2014) – agrees:

> Research into play deprivation reveals that children significantly deprived of opportunities to play are more likely to be aggressive, repress emotions, lack social skills and have an increased tendency towards obesity. 'Chronic, long term deprivation results in depression, withdrawal and decreased neuro-endocrine activity in the brain and nervous system'. If children don't play they suffer.

Non-directive play therapists have long known this and strive to create and resource an environment and to give that space and set times to children who need to understand and work out their difficult experiences for themselves. Very much like the model above, the play therapist respectfully gives safe control of the playing over to the child and sensitively supports that as it unfolds, carefully watching and listening, participating when invited and ensuring the most helpful resources are available. 'The model of therapist as superior being is not appropriate if we wish the child to explore and make sense of their world through play' (Cattanach 1994:52). Adults who wish to support children's play need to flatten the usual hierarchy so that children feel the power of that equal regard, giving them freedom to control their playing.

Ali has told this next story elsewhere (Wood cited in Brown 2014: 90), but it is highly appropriate here as an example of how with the permissive support and the right props, children will play out their prior experiences in order to understand them and gain mastery over them.

Periodically I used to go to a local authority open-access playcentre, where I knew the playworkers well, to observe and reflect on playing and be a spare pair of hands when needed. On this occasion I had not met Alex (not his real name) before. He was six, in foster care and had started coming regularly to the centre. He had little speech and an awkward gait, a big happy smile and on this occasion was full of enthusiasm. He came over to me soon after his arrival, took my hand and urged me to go outside. With me following his lead, we trotted and skipped about the playground, waving our arms and making all kinds of noises and laughing at our antics.

After several traversals of the playground, Alex urged me to follow him into the playhouse – a garden shed with windows, curtains and a big dressing up box. We went in and started rifling through the clothes and props. Alex suddenly stood up, shut the curtains and firmly shut the door. He then turned round and his face had totally changed. I can only describe it as menacing. I watched him carefully wondering where we were going next.

He started to laugh in this menacing way, while clearly looking through the box for something. He found it – a leather belt – and then started to shout excitedly at me. I began to wonder what he might be playing out, so I played along, pretending to cower for a while, but he then got even more agitated and came over to me putting the belt around my neck.

It was one of those moments when you call on your instinct and hope it's an appropriate response. As he started to pull the belt tighter, I changed tack and said firmly, 'No, I don't want to play this game anymore' and freed myself from the belt. Alex's face immediately broke into an expression of relief and he threw his arms around me. I hugged him back, thinking I had no idea what had just happened, but feeling sure it was quite significant to Alex. He then took my hand again, opened the door and we proceeded to run round the playground again as before, but this time we sang made-up songs at the tops of our voices and he seemed full of happiness. He then stopped and moved away from me to play something else and he ignored me for the rest of the session, but when his foster mum came to collect him, he ran over to me and gave me a brief hug and a sunny smile before going home.

I spoke later to the senior playworkers, relaying what had happened. They told me his foster mum had told them that Alex had been discovered at two years old tied to his cot by a belt around his neck. It was thought he had never left the cot as he was unable to walk. He was immediately taken into care and four years later, was still 'catching up' on his lost early development.

I was more than a little shaken. We reflected for a while on what had happened and discussed a number of possible future considerations and strategies (he had not behaved like this before). I hoped and hoped that my instinctive response was an empowering one for him as he played out the aggressor and re-enacted his experience, but this time with the victim taking control. What had sparked that playing that day, and why me? I'll never know, but I remain in awe at the power and potential of play.

It would have been so easy to have stopped that play episode with Alex much earlier by telling him to 'play nicely' – a phrase that rolls off so many of our tongues when we see children playing aggressively, using language we don't like or touching on themes and topics that make us uncomfortable. But this is normal for children when playing – it is what they do. Fisher gives a lovely story (2016:65–7) about an early educator being invited to play with a group of boys intent on lasering the baddies and really getting into the spirit of it with them, giving her instructions on recognizing enemy aliens and which imaginary buttons to press on her 'laser'. She remarks,

> The children involved in this play do not respond to an indoor, more static environment. They prefer the freedom of the outdoors and the opportunity to develop their own self-initiated play. By inviting the teacher into the play they are showing a great deal of respect and affection. They know, from previous experience, that she will join in and enhance their play, not condemn it (because it is 'gun play') or try and take it over (because it doesn't have her objectives). The teacher remains absolutely engaged in the storytelling throughout. By joining in and following their lead, the teacher creates a strong relationship with the boys that will spill over into more formal, perhaps more sedentary, learning situations when the need arises. She will know more about the boys' interests and will use them as a 'hook' for the learning that she

leads. The freedom of the environment in which the boys are playing allows them to be creative and imaginative and helps them improve their social skills as they negotiate and act out their story.

Similar research by Holland (2003) and Katch (2001) illustrates how the violent themes in children's play are necessary for them on many levels and in keeping with Playwork Principle 7 (PPSG 2005) 'playworkers recognise their own impact on the play space and also the impact of children and young people's play on the playworker', they encourage us to understand children better – and judge them less – by developing an awareness of our own reactions and feelings and reining these in before we respond. Children's play will involve games of power, gender, bias and exclusion (Grieshaber and McCardle 2010) in order to make sense of their world, and so sensitive attention to and unobtrusive observation of their playing will help us understand this and support them better.

Children do indeed experience a range of emotions and move on in making sense of these when they play, as we have seen through the stories and examples in this chapter. The role of the attending adult, if there is one, is also clearly important. The adult needs to 'tune in' to the child and their interests, needs and agendas, if we are to be of service to them – even when the adult also has an agenda that must be addressed. The following story is a lovely example of one such sensitive adult working at Great Ormond Street Children's Hospital, who went the extra mile in ensuring that a child with leukaemia could still play in the way he wanted and needed.

> *Daniel had a diagnosis of Acute Lymphoblastic Leukaemia (ALL) only a few weeks after his first birthday. For the next two years he would be required to undergo intensive chemotherapy which would hopefully cure his leukaemia. In the process, however, his immune system would be significantly impacted, sometimes being so affected that he would need to avoid all activities normal for a child his age including mixing with other children at toddler groups and at times not being able to play freely in the garden, on the beach or at the park due to the risk of infection.*
>
> *He would also be admitted to hospital multiple times between courses of chemotherapy due to neutropenia – a state that occurs when an individual's white blood cell counts are extremely low – causing opportunistic infections and fevers and requiring supplementary courses of IV antibiotics.*
>
> *During these hospital admissions, Daniel would be cared for in a side room and would be unable to freely wander along to the ward playroom. His depleted immune system would mean that playing alongside other children or accessing toys that had not first been thoroughly cleaned would be too risky to his health.*

Instead, play activities would need to be brought to him by a health play specialist (HPS).

When Daniel was 2 and a half years old, he was admitted to hospital because he was neutropenic and had developed an infection, requiring IV antibiotics. When the HPS went to see the family and ask Daniel what he would like to play today, his mother expressed sadness and frustration that both at home and in hospital she could not seem to help him play in the way he had been enjoying before his last round of chemotherapy or provide him activities that he seemed to happily 'get lost in', saying, 'He just wants to dig!' She also explained that he could not even just go and dig in the garden at home due to the risk of infection.

In a similar way, sand is a difficult substance for use in play in a hospital setting. This is partly due to the way it is sourced, stored and played with, meaning it may harbour bacteria and cannot ever be assumed to be 'clean'. It can also very easily infiltrate dressings, wounds and IV access devices. As a result, many children's wards avoid using sand altogether. In Daniel's case, safety concerns about his permanent intravenous access (a Hickman line) and infection control policies in place at the hospital meant that simply sourcing and providing Daniel with a quantity of sand was not possible for the HPS either. His desire and request to dig was going to be a bit of a challenge.

In the absence of sand, sometimes water play or another type of messy play might be considered for children like Daniel. However, the HPS had noticed on previous occasions that Daniel showed an aversion to messy play finding them uncomfortable and overwhelming. Knowing this, the HPS was determined to find a dry substance which was acceptable to Daniel but would allow him to dig, explore and play freely.

Where the safety and stability of sand and soil is not suitable for children in hospital, there are still options – particularly food-based options that would not necessarily automatically be considered play materials, but which lend themselves brilliantly to becoming a substitute for sand due to their texture. Using a mixture of crushed cereal, dry rice and red lentils the HPS enabled Daniel to have a fairly big quantity of 'special sand' which was taken to his room in a tray with a selection of digging implements. The texture was unfamiliar but it was still acceptable to Daniel because it was dry. With some playful support by the HPS he was reassured and encouraged to explore it at his own pace with a spade and his fingers.

Trucks were then added to the tray and 'special sand' as well as some small world figures, some shells and some large-sized plastic gems for Daniel to find in among the 'sand', adding further richness to the experience of play. With the HPS giving space for Daniel to explore freely while remaining present and by his side, he soon became accustomed to the texture, smell (and even the taste!) of the substitute sand and was able to enjoy digging, sprinkling and driving trucks through it for a fairly long period of time. Hubbuck 2020

Without the input of the HPS giving consideration to Daniel's play needs and preferences, his development, as well as the effects and limitations of his cancer diagnosis, his ability to play in hospital would have been severely limited to whatever toys had been brought in a hospital bag by his parents. Their ability to tune in to Daniel and recognize what he needed enabled him to play in a way that was enjoyable, open-ended, exploratory and challenging (from a sensory perspective) without being overwhelming or endangering his health.

Where does this leave us? We have told stories from a range of settings and different professionals that illustrate the emotional content of play and give some responses from the adults who were there – all of whom, knowingly or unknowingly, used the playwork approach in supporting the children in these stories. Recognizing the power of play in emotional regulation and building resilience and therefore giving time, space, freedom and materials to children together with sensitive support can be part of any professional practice as well as that of playworkers. We would argue that embedding training on this for all those working with children in health, education and care would generate a more universal response and increase reflective practice across the children's workforce. 'Play is a child's life and the means by which he comes to understand the world he lives in' (Isaacs cited in Cattanach 2008:35) – we owe it to all children everywhere to ensure they can freely play.

8
Health and Well-being

Chapter Outline

Play's relationship to healthy development and well-being

If you were asked what the word 'health' meant to you, what would your answer be? In Article 24 of the UN Convention on the Rights of the Child (UNICEF 1989) health is identified as a right, and every child has the right to the best possible health. We know that health is important and very significant in people's lives, but what is it actually? Health is a complex, multidimensional and subjective concept (Green et al. 2019). Despite some common baselines, what being healthy or unhealthy means for one person, including children and young people, will be different from what it means to other people. The different meanings of health held by different people will be influenced by where they live and the resources available to them. Underdown (2007) gives the example of a child from a poor family living in sub-Saharan Africa during a famine being viewed as healthy by their community because they are free of disease and relatively well nourished, but how in a more prosperous country there would be different expectations for the child to be viewed as healthy.

Green et al. (2019) comment that the task of defining health has been compared with shovelling smoke. The difficulty and complexity of this task is demonstrated in how the definition of health by the World Health Organization (WHO) has evolved over time. Underdown (2007) comments that in 1948 the definition of health proposed by WHO stated, 'Health is a state of complete physical, mental and social well-being and not merely the absence of disease'. This definition emphasized *being well* rather than *not being ill* and demonstrated a basic view of health by referring to mental and social well-being as well as physical health. However, it was criticized for suggesting a perfect state of health which is potentially unachievable and unrealistic (Blaxter 2010). To reflect a more achievable and realistic definition, the WHO (1986) expanded their definition adding,

> To reach a state of complete physical, mental and social well-being, an individual or group must be able to identify and to realize aspirations, to satisfy needs, and to change or cope with the environment. Health is, therefore, seen as a resource for everyday life, not the objective of living. Health is a positive concept emphasizing social and personal resources, as well as physical capacities.

This addition takes a holistic view of health while also recognizing there may be limitations to achieving it, requiring people to adapt to their environment. In the 'Moving into the Future' section, the charter even mentions play, stating that 'Health is created and lived by people within the settings of their everyday life; where they learn, work, play and love'. Alexander, Frohlich and Fusco (2014) suggest that this reference to play is important as it acknowledges the significant contribution play makes to children's overall health and well-being.

Entangled with the complexity of defining what health is, is the use of the term 'well-being', which is often, as with the title of this chapter, used in conjunction with health. In some literature 'well-being' is used interchangeably with the term 'health', but in other sources it has a subtly different meaning, such as referring only to emotional health or being used as shorthand for just the positive aspects of health (Green et al. 2019). The concept of well-being and especially how it is used in research has been criticized for being individualistic, presented as something that individuals possess which can and should be achieved, placing the responsibility for their well-being on the individual and disregarding the impact of other issues (Russell, Barclay and Tawil, 2023) such as access to resources. Authors such as Lester (2020) have raised concerns about how the concept of well-being is interpreted and used, especially in policy related to children. He suggests that it often reflects a deficit approach, where well-being is measured in terms of 'a lack of something' (ibid:90) reflecting the priorities of political parties rather than actual lived experiences.

Russell, Barclay and Tawil (2023) suggest that using a relational capability approach can offer new ways of thinking about children's play and well-being. Relating to the posthumanist approach mentioned in Chapters 4 and 5 and children's capabilities mentioned in Chapters 2 and 7, this approach emphasizes moving away from viewing childhood and play as static, viewing them instead as being continually co-produced, changing and evolving through their entanglements and encounters with other aspects. Well-being within this approach is viewed not as being fixed and located inside the bodies and minds of individual children but rather as fluctuating and emerging through entanglements.

If we are involved in supporting children and young people's play, it is important that we reflect on what being healthy or unhealthy means to us, as well as our understanding of well-being (and the views of others we work with), as this may influence what is made available or not available to them. Our views on health can influence our view of play and how we value different types of play. Likewise, our views on play can influence what we think of as healthy or unhealthy. As shown in the example, there may be types of play that we have concerns about because we feel they encourage unhealthy behaviour or may have a potentially negative effect on children and young people's health.

In a discussion about buying presents, Bob mentioned feeling uncomfortable when his eight-year-old nephew asked for a computer game. While he wanted to buy him what he wanted, he was not sure about buying him a computer game, feeling that this would only encourage more screen time, which he thought was unhealthy.

This example raises questions about certain kinds of play, or ways of playing, such as digital play being viewed by adults as unhealthy (we make further reference to this in Chapter 6). Bob, in the example, is not alone in having concerns about children playing computer games increasing their screen time and sedentary behaviour. Concerns have been raised about the impact increased screen time has on children and young people's eyesight both by play practitioners and authors (Kingston-Hughes 2022) and health professionals (Pardhan et al. 2022). This has been especially apparent during the pandemic, which saw lockdowns increasing screen time due to school lessons being delivered online and children and young people's opportunities to play and socialize outdoors being restricted. While increased screen time has been linked to various adverse health conditions such as eyesight problems, increase in obesity, lack of sleep and physical activity, it also enabled many children and young people (and adults as well) to feel less socially isolated during the pandemic through being able to connect to and play with others online (Tambalis et al. 2020).

As Judith, a teenager, doing her GCSEs during the pandemic, reflected

If I hadn't had my computer during lockdown, I don't know what I would have done. I might have gone mad. Not only did I need it for school, but it meant that I could play games with my friends online. There wasn't much else

we could do during the lockdowns. You could go for a walk, but that was about it. People talk about too much screen time, but during the lockdowns, everyone had more screen time. Covid-19 was a much bigger risk to our health.

During the lockdowns in England, the rules were that people could only go outdoors for physical exercise once a day, and Judith mentions feeling that she could only be outdoors if she was going for a walk. Gill and Miller (2020) commented that the term *physical exercise* was often interpreted in a restrictive way during the pandemic and did not acknowledge that for children, their play is their physical exercise. With fines being put in place for breaches of the rules, people worried about what they were allowed or not allowed to do outdoors. Thinking back to the lockdowns and the rules about going outdoors for exercise once a day, Stanley, a parent, reflected.

We are a large family anyway, so when we went out for a walk and passed other people who didn't know us, sometimes they would look at us and we would wonder if they were thinking that we were breaking the rules. It made us feel uncomfortable to be outdoors sometimes, as if we were being watched all the time and checked on to see if we were following the rules. It wasn't a nice atmosphere at times. We'd often take a ball with us just to make it a bit more fun, but then, when we were laughing and playing around with the ball, I worried that this wouldn't be viewed as going out for physical exercise and that we weren't taking the lockdown rules seriously. Looking back, it seems weird that I felt like this. Of course, playing with a ball is ok, but those were strange days. Everyday things that we took for granted suddenly didn't seem okay anymore.

The UK government has concerns about the links between children's reduced levels of physical activity, increased sedentary lifestyles and obesity, and several health programmes have been initiated to encourage children and young people to be more physically active and eat more healthily. One programme, current at the time of writing, is the Holiday Activities and Food programme (HAF) (GOV.UK 2022). This programme offers provision of free holiday clubs for children in receipt of free school meals through school holiday periods with the aim of encouraging healthy eating, increased physical activity and developing 'resilience, character and well being along with their wider educational attainment through enrichment activities' (GOV.UK 2022). Holiday clubs are required to provide activities that enable children to engage on average in sixty minutes per day in moderate to vigorous physical activity, which can be through free play.

It is good that free play, play which children choose to engage in for its own sake, as proposed by the playwork approach, is recognized in the HAF programme as being beneficial for children's health and development. There is reference to the programme developing well-being and resilience, but this appears to be more through the enrichment activities rather than through play, with the focus on play being used to increase children's physical activity. Alexander, Frohlich and Fusco (2012) suggest that when play is used in this way in health promotion programmes, it misses the opportunity to fully recognize the value of play for children's social and emotional development and promote health in a more holistic way.

So, what is play's relationship to children's healthy development and well-being? Kilvington and Wood (2016) suggest that ideas about the benefits of play for children's development can be grouped into two schools of thought: deferred and immediate benefits. The idea of deferred benefits refers to play's benefits being future-focused, helping children to become better adults, whereas the idea of immediate benefits emphasizes the benefits for children in the present time, the here and now. Play's role in children's health and development has been recognized across multiple disciplines with different benefits being identified depending on how play is understood. The American Academy of Pediatrics, in their report *The Power of Play*, recommend that paediatricians become advocates for the protection of children's unstructured play because of its health and development benefits. For example, they suggest play supports children to manage stress, form nurturing relationships with parents and carers, and can have lifelong benefits in preventing obesity, hypertension and type 2 diabetes through the development of motor skills. They recommend a 'prescription for play' should be written at every well-child visit in the first two years of a child's life (Yogman et al. 2018:10).

To support this recommendation, the LEGO Foundation has developed the Prescription for Play (P4P) programme for healthcare providers in the United States to use when seeing children aged eighteen to thirty-six months. The programme offers free packs containing LEGO DUPLO® bricks and a brochure for parents and carers on the importance and benefits of play for children. The aim of the programme is to promote the value of play for the children and encourage parents and carers to actively engage in play with their child (Panjwani et al. 2022). A review of the impact of this programme identified that it developed healthcare providers, parents and carers' understanding about the benefits of play for children's health and led to an increase in the amount of time each week parents and carers played with their children (Panjwani et al. 2022).

The importance of child-led outdoor play for physical, social and emotional development has been recognized by health organizations in the UK such as NHS Gloucestershire. NHS Gloucestershire works in partnership with Play Gloucestershire, a registered charity which enables opportunities for active and creative outdoor play, to support children and young people's mental health (Play Gloucestershire, 2021). One programme offered by Play Gloucestershire to schools and other organizations is Play Nurture, which enables children affected by adverse childhood experiences to have the time and space for child-led outdoor play. This enables the children to experience the therapeutic benefits of outdoor play for developing healthy ways to cope with life's stresses and enhancing their emotional well-being (Gloucestershire Healthy Living and Learning 2023, Play Gloucestershire 2023).

NHS Birmingham and Solihull in the West Midlands UK are currently embarking on a pilot project giving grant funding to five voluntary organizations working with children and young people who can offer support with backlogs and waiting lists by offering playful and enrichment activities. GPs and other medical professionals will refer families to these organizations by offering social prescriptions to parents, in recognition that play supports the well-being of children and families.

Another example of partnership work between a health and a play organization to support children and young people's mental health through play is found at Meriden Adventure Playground. Joint weekly therapeutic play sessions are delivered by the adventure playground staff and psychologists from the Child and Adolescent Mental Health Services (CAMHS) team for children on their caseloads with mental health issues.

Clair, a researcher at the playground, reflects on the children's experiences of these sessions in relation to their well-being.

Kai makes 'sensory balls' with sand/punch balloons. He makes several and names each one. Returning to the playground a few days later, he walks on site exclaiming loudly, 'Look, sensory 4 and 5 are still alive!' For the children attending this group, there is a 'history' of making sensory items at the playground, and they know that their need to do so is responded to, both playfully and seriously by staff members. The children often return and talk about taking these items into their classroom or other settings to combat anxiety.

The developmental perspective on play focuses on the usefulness of play for children's development, emphasizing how children develop socially, physically, emotionally and intellectually through play (Nijhof 2018). Jarvis (2019:6) suggests that within this perspective, play is viewed as 'a flexible self-directed experience which serves the needs both of the individual child, and of the future society in which s/he will live in adulthood'. Within this perspective, children's play is valued for its instrumental value (Powell 2009) and its usefulness for achieving outcomes. Adults will offer activities to guide or enhance children's development and may limit or stop play they feel has no developmental benefits (Brown and Cheesman 2003).

Research has indicated that play is important for healthy brain development (Frost, Wortham and Reifel 2012). For ethical reasons, previous research exploring the relationship between play and healthy brain development has been conducted on animals as it often involved invasive surgical procedures. Pellis and Pellis's research into rough and tumble play and play with objects of animals such as mice and rats spans over thirty years (Pellis and Pellis 2009). Their studies have provided evidence of the impact on brain development in specific areas of the pre-frontal cortex and of poor levels of social competence in animals deprived of play opportunities (Pellis et al. 2006). Panksepp's (1998) research into rats identified systems at a subcortical level in the brain which encourage play, which were found to promote brain development and socialization. These studies are often cited as demonstrating that play is important for healthy child brain development, and it is possible that this is the case, but as Lester and Russell (2008) advise, we need to be careful of applying the findings from these controlled laboratory experiments on animals to humans. The very varied understandings of what play is, across the disciplines as referred to in Chapter 1, need to be considered in relation to these findings.

The development of non-intrusive methods of brain imaging, such as functional near-infrared spectroscopy (FNIRS), a wearable hat-type piece of equipment, has enabled research to be carried out with children to explore and measure brain activity during play. Hashmi et al. (2022) used it to capture changes in brain activity as children played with dolls or games on tablet devices on their own and with a partner. They found that during doll play, children referred to their emotions and thoughts much more than when they were using tablet devices, and the social processing areas of the brain were more active.

Liu et al. (2017) reviewed evidence of the value of play in relation to brain development and identified five characteristics of playful experiences:

- Joy – is essential for neural networks needed for cognitive development and learning. Joy increases dopamine levels in the brain's reward system, which enhance memory, attention, creativity and motivation.
- Meaningfulness – introduces new things which the brain can make connections to, linking them to things that are already familiar. This process develops networks in the brain associated with analogical

thinking (identifying similarities), memory, transfer, metacognition (understanding one's own thought processes), creating insight, motivation and reward.
- Actively engaging -- involves the brain using networks which enhance memory encoding and retrieval processes, decision-making and agency (having control over actions and consequences).
- Iterative thinking – involves repeatedly processing information, which engages networks in the brain facilitating flexible thinking, understanding alternative viewpoints, perseverance, and is linked to reward and memory networks that underpin learning.
- Socially interactive – positive social interactions promote plasticity in the brain, building neural foundations for developing healthy social regulation and protection from stress. Social interaction activates brain networks which enable detecting the mental state of others, which is important for gaining insight and learning.

Figure 8.1 Playing Basecamp. 2023. Courtesy of Wu.

Their findings illustrate how these characteristics, all of which we would argue occur during play, enable the development and activation of interconnected brain processes in growing children and support their capacity to learn.

Thinking about the role of the adult in relation to supporting children's play, play will in many different contexts be initiated by adults and children often enjoy and benefit from this kind of play, especially when the adult is attuned to their interests. The 'Basecamp' game is a good example of this. This is a game Sarah made up for her daughter and two cousins who were staying with them (but you will probably recognize this type of game and may have played some kind of version of it yourself).

So, you agree on a spot that is the Basecamp which is protected by one person. This person has to find the others before they get to Basecamp. The others use the walkie-talkies (see Figures 8.1 and 8.2) *to share intelligence, such as where the path is clear, to help each other get to the Basecamp and not get caught.*

The other game they like is 'Take me to prison'. I wrap them up in a big blanket and move it around, so it feels like they have been captured and are going on a bumpy road to jail. I think that is Daisy's favourite, but she is getting a bit big now!

Julia has seen the Basecamp game in action and observed how much enjoyment the children got out of it. The 'Take me to prison' game results in the children howling with laughter. From a developmental perspective (Jarvis 2019) the Basecamp game can be viewed as being useful for developing the children's physical skills, as they are physically active, having to move stealthily through the environment to avoid detection or if playing the 'Basecamp protector' move around to detect the others, and running to the Basecamp in order to get there before being caught or to protect it from invaders. The children are developing their social skills by playing by the rules of the game, developing strategies to win, as well as those trying to get to the Basecamp cooperating and working together. They are developing their observation and listening skills and learning about waiting, managing anticipation and suspense. From an educational perspective on play (Brock 2019) the children are problem-solving, learning about the space of the environment as they plan their routes to get to the Basecamp and having to change these plans if the Basecamp protector starts heading their way. They are developing their communication, language and technology skills through using the walkie-talkies to send each other messages. From a playwork perspective, the emphasis would be on children's choice, the children having the opportunity to freely adapt the rules and take the game where they wanted to, because

Figure 8.2 Playing Basecamp undercover. 2023. Courtesy of Wu.

while the game may have been initiated by an adult, the play belongs to the children and not the adult. As mentioned in Chapter 5, the playworker's role is to co-create the space, creating the conditions for play.

Brett, a sports coach, reflects on his experience of using the playwork approach in his practice.

At times, I have been so regimented in my practice that the fun element of sports has been lost in the pursuit of technical development, and I have often found myself being criticized by the young people that I am too strict! Although they felt comfortable enough to confront me.

One game that particularly stood out was a variation of football, and they named the game after me as a tribute, which was very touching. I allowed the class to choose what game they wanted to do for their final lesson, and they chose Brett Ball. I took part in this session, and it was fun and engaging. I was proud of the pupils as they had invented and delivered their own game and rules.

This approach has changed my coaching style, and now I always allow for pupils to shape the sessions. Through this approach, you see lots of development take place, such as teamwork, cooperation, communication, leadership, analytic thinking and learning through exploring, trial and error.

The playwork approach has allowed me and participants to create stronger bonds, increase engagement, motivation and enthusiasm and develop other valuable life skills.

As previously mentioned in Chapter 1, Playwork Principles 1 and 2 (PPSG 2005) establish how play is viewed within the playwork approach. It is the emphasis on understanding play as a process, a journey without there needing to be a destination (although there might be, it is up to the child), an experience, a moment, all without there needing to be an end result or outcome, that sets the playwork approach apart from other perspectives on play which focus on the instrumental value of play (Powell 2009). In those perspectives, play is valued for its usefulness for achieving something else, such as a learning or developmental outcome. Children's play is justified by what it can achieve rather than play being valued for play's sake. While recognizing the potential long-term benefits of playing, the playwork approach emphasizes the immediate benefits of play for children's healthy development and well-being in the present time, the here and now.

However, some adults find it difficult to view play as a process without having an end result. They may feel uncomfortable about giving children the freedom to play as they want to and feel an urge to direct the children's play. They may feel out of control or like a spare part when children are playing and do not need any adult involvement. Brown (2015) suggests that this is a key aspect that differentiates the playwork approach from other professions, that the child's agenda is at the centre of their practice. Other professions may work in the interests of the child but have their own agendas, and these agendas may form habits of practice that are difficult to let go of, as Mary recalls, thinking back to her first day working as a playworker after having been a teacher.

I had been a primary school teacher with a specialism in art, and I was asked by a friend to work on their summer playscheme. I thought this sounded like fun and spent the time before the job started planning lots of exciting art projects for the children. On my first day, I spent time setting up an arts and crafts table with lots of different art materials for the children to use. I knew enough about the playwork approach not to make children come and 'do art' but instead of finding the experience fun, I found that I was on edge and anxious. I was anxious when there weren't any children using the art materials because I felt like I wasn't doing anything and that would give the wrong impression to the other workers. Finally, when some children did come and start painting, I found myself wanting to guide them and show them the right way to mix colours, so everything didn't turn into a mucky brown. The children didn't care that it had turned into a mucky brown; in fact they seemed to like it. One child, instead of painting on the paper I had put out for them, started painting the palm of their hand and I didn't know what to do because that's not what I had had in mind when I set the arts and crafts table up.

Alexander, Frohlich and Fusco (2012) suggest that free play, rather than goal-orientated, adult-guided play or activities, may be exactly the kind of opportunity that has the potential to promote health in a more holistic way. Do you agree that allowing children to paint in any way they choose was better for their well-being than trying to instruct them? If so, why?

The benefits of free play rather than adult-initiated activities are not always recognized by all adults, as the story from Sarah, a playworker at Pitsmoor Adventure Playground, shows.

Looking across the adventure playground, several children were playing with a tarpaulin. They had turned it into a parachute. They had measured how big the tarpaulin was by measuring it using their own bodies. They hid from a playworker underneath it. They made a den out of it and found items from around the playground to use to furnish it. Inside the building, children were making and creating models with playdough. Other children were painting freely on large pieces of cardboard. A young child was showing a playworker the 'Biscuit Bandit' they had drawn with chalks to warn them about what it looked like. Another playworker had been requested by the children to help them plant some bulbs in pots so they could take them home. Several children were shrieking in joy as they whizzed down the zip wire together. Across the playground, six different ball games were taking place. Two children sat at opposite sides of a table, elbows placed carefully on the table, hands gripped as they arm-wrestled. A group of children had gathered up sheets of A4 paper and were folding them carefully to make paper aeroplanes which they threw in the air to see whose design would fly the furthest. Children were chasing each other in a game of tag. Paper and crayons were available for children to help themselves. A parent came up to a playworker and asked, 'Are you putting on any activities today?'

This question from the parent raises some interesting points about what different adults value children doing. The parent did not appear to see any value in the free play that was happening in the adventure playground, or perhaps they did not even notice what was going on? Their interest was in what adult-initiated activities would be put on for the children. Why might this be? The children are playing in an adventure playground, which operates the 'three frees' ethos (Conway 2009:4); free to enter, there is no charge to play there, children are free to play how they wish (within guidelines for safe behaviour) and are (aged eight to thirteen years) free to come and go as they please. So, the parent's comment is not about value for money but about something else; about what the staff within the setting will be 'putting on' for the children, what adult-initiated activities would be available. This reveals some key points about adults' perceptions about the value of play and the role adults have in relation to supporting children's play.

What free play offers in comparison with adult-directed play or activities is choice, control and more opportunities to be creative, imaginative and experimental (Smith and Pellegrini 2005). Lester (2018) suggests that playing itself is a pleasurable expression of being well. Unstructured freely chosen play contributes to children's mental health and well-being through enabling children to have the freedom to choose and to experience challenge (Manwaring and Taylor 2007).

Let's examine the playing that is happening in the previous example from the adventure playground in relation to what this offers for children's health and well-being. In relation to the five characteristics of playful experiences that were identified by Liu et al. (2017) as being significant for brain development, Sarah mentions joy, that the children on the zip wire are *shrieking in joy.* Meaningfulness is demonstrated by the children trying out new things with the tarpaulin, first turning it into a parachute, then measuring it with their bodies, developing their mathematical understanding, then using it to hide from a playworker and then finally making a den out of it. The children are actively engaging with the resources available to them in the playground, not only with the tarpaulin but also with playdough, pieces of cardboard, paper, and with each other and with the playworkers. Iterative thinking is indicated in the way that the children adapt their use of the tarpaulin and in the development of the designs of the paper aeroplanes to create one that flew the furthest. The children are socially interacting; they are playing together with various resources, they are chasing each other, they are hiding from a playworker, they are sharing a drawing with a playworker and explaining its meaning and they are asking a playworker to help them. The children are being physically active, they are involved in different ball games, planting bulbs, enjoying the thrill of whizzing down a zip wire and testing their strength by arm-wrestling. If we return to the WHO (1986) definition of health as a 'positive concept emphasizing social and personal resources, as well as physical capacities', we can see that, in the adventure playground, children are developing their social and personal resources, as well as their physical capacities.

When we think of health in relation to children's play, we often think of it in connection with safety, physical safety (as opposed to well-being); making sure that where the children are playing is a safe space and that any potential hazards, things that could cause harm, have been assessed for the likelihood of potentially causing harm. Chapter 6 explored the playwork perspective on hazards, risks and resilience in relation to children's play and their well-being.

Playwork Principle 2 (PPSG 2005) states, 'Play is a process that is freely chosen, personally directed and intrinsically motivated. That is, children and young people determine and control the content and intent of their play, by following their own instincts, ideas and interests, in their own way for their own reasons'. To support this understanding of play in practice, adults need to recognize that children's play may involve themes that we are personally uncomfortable with, such as death, which may cause us a dilemma. Do we support children to explore these themes in their play by creating a safe space for them to do so? Or do we stop or try to interrupt and change the play to something we are more comfortable with?

Olusoga (2019:75) shares a story from Elisabeth, a nursery worker, which raises just such a dilemma.

Julia was still very new to nursery and was in the home corner exploring the equipment, but generally not interacting with the other children around her. After some time, she picked up a doll, wrapped it in a blanket and held it to her chest. Then, with her other hand, she picked up one of the telephones and began frantically dialling. At this point, I moved away from the area to support some other children using construction. After some moments, I became aware that Julia was shouting. As I looked up, she was still 'on the phone', but was shouting for the police to come and arrest her husband before he hurt someone. Her language at this point included a number of pretty hardcore swear words. Other children around her had stopped what they were doing and were staring at her. I went to Julia and interrupted her play, asking her to come and do some painting with me. I was concerned not only about the other children hearing the language she was using and repeating it but at the heightened emotional state Julia appeared to be in. Julia came and painted with me and then went on to paint by herself at the easel. At break, as I was discussing the incident with my nursery nurse, a teaching assistant who lived near Julia came in and told us that the previous night the police had been called to Julia's house, and her dad had been arrested. Afterwards, Julia's mum had told neighbours that she had called the police because he had become violent towards her and had hit her while she was holding her baby son.

What would you have done in such a situation? Would you have interrupted Julia's play, or let her continue? What would you be most concerned about? The theme of her play? Her emotional state? That she was using hardcore swear words? That other children had stopped playing and were staring at her? Would you be worried about the effect that Julia's play might have on the other children? Would you be concerned that the other children might repeat the swear words they had heard at home, and this would lead to complaints from their parents?

From a playwork perspective, which focuses on supporting the play process, Julia should be able to be in control of the content and intent of her play, as it is through play that she is trying to revisit her memory and make sense of the traumatic experience she has had. She needs a safe space to be able to do this, and this may be the only place she feels safe enough to do this in. If we view her play as her way of communicating, then an adult stopping her play can give her the message that they do not want to listen to what she wants to say and that they are not able to cope with what she has to say. As mentioned in Chapter 5, playworkers support all children in creating a space in which they can play. In this story with Julia, the challenge is how to enable her to have a safe space to play without it negatively impacting on other children's play. How this is made possible will depend on the space, resources and staffing level of the setting where it occurs. For example, in some settings, it might be possible to offer the other children a different space to play in, to enable Julia time and space to continue playing.

An area of children's development that adults may feel uncomfortable supporting in their play or even acknowledging is their sexual development. Working with children and young people, we will be familiar with safeguarding and being aware of the signs and indicators of abuse and will be alert to children's behaviour that potentially indicates they are experiencing sexual abuse. However, this is different from children exploring their own sexual development in their play. This is an area of play that only a few playwork authors explore, for example Kilvington and Wood (2016) and Else (2009, 2014). In reviewing Hughes's (2002) play types, Else (2009) and Kilvington and Wood (2018) have questioned whether there are more play types still to be classified and wonder if sexual play may be one of the missing ones. This form of play involves children and young people responding to changes in their bodies, emerging feelings and exploring relationships and roles with others who are different sexes or the same sex (Else 2009). Else (2009) suggests that this type of play is frequently viewed as a taboo subject with adults often feeling threatened or embarrassed by it, leading them to either stop it or intervene to change the content. He comments that if this play occurs between children, then adults should not feel compelled to intervene. He refers to commonplace games such as 'mummies and daddies' and 'Kiss Chase' as ways that children explore different social and emotional roles. Kilvington and Wood (2016) suggest that sexual play is a common phenomenon among many children which is primarily motivated by curiosity. In supporting children's play process and creating safe spaces for children to try out 'what ifs' and different roles and relationships, do we draw the line at supporting children's sexual development and their sexual play?

Lester (2020:114) suggests that playing 'is children's way of co-creating their own health resources, not something given to them from outside their *milieux*'. As Sutton-Smith (1997:32) suggests 'play for children, quite simply makes children happier'. The playwork approach to health and well-being can be seen as a supportive role to enable children to have time and space to play freely.

9
Gender

Chapter Outline

Children and gender and gendered play

In this chapter, we are going to explore play and playwork through the lens of gender. We will touch on how evolution, society, local and national cultures affect how children are expected to perform their gender in relation to their sex, but for much of the chapter, we will look at how children approach gender and sexuality in their lives and through the medium of play. We will take notice of children's expressed views on the topic.

First, we will outline what we mean by certain terms. We use the word **gender** to describe 'our awareness and reaction to our assigned biological sex, which is influenced by biological, psychological, and social factors' (Kilvington and Wood 2016:17). This is not the same as a **gender identity**, which according to the HRC Foundation (n.d.) is 'One's innermost concept of self as male, female, a blend of both or neither – how individuals perceive themselves and what they call themselves. One's gender identity can be the same or different from the sex assigned at birth'. **Gender expression or performance** is the external appearance of one's gender, usually expressed through behaviour, clothing, haircut, voice, choice of activity and so on, and which may or may not conform to socially defined behaviours and characteristics typically associated with being either masculine or feminine and may or may not be in line with the internal gender identity. This may, to a large extent, depend on the reactions of other adults and children to atypical gender behavioural expectations. **Masculinity** and **femininity** are used in relation to stereotypical traits and roles generally associated with men and women within the class, racial and ethnic culture that they live in. National factors also have a bearing on expectations of behaviour. At one time masculine and feminine were considered opposites, but that idea is now outmoded.

When we refer to **sex** we will be talking about whether a person is considered male or female based on the visible and internal biological structures that a baby is born with. However, it is now realized that not everybody is quite as they appear to be externally because of biological differences in their hormones or internal organs. Also, not everybody is happy with being identified as male or female based on their physical attributes, and they may feel like or wish to be a different sex or neither. **Transgender** is an umbrella term for those people whose gender identity and/or expression is different from cultural expectations based on the sex they were assigned at birth. This may include people considering themselves transgender, non-binary, gender fluid or agender, plus an evolving list of descriptive words. Being transgender does not imply any specific sexual orientation. Therefore, transgender people may identify as straight, gay, lesbian, bisexual and so on.

Figure 9.1 Role reversal? 2022. Courtesy of Delaney.

According to the US Guide for Early Childhood Programs and Professionals (n.d.), the age at which gender identity becomes established varies from as young as two and for others it may be fluid until adolescence or beyond. Sexual orientation emerges during childhood, adolescence or later in life. Child experts, such as Bryan (2012), suggest it is not possible to predict what a child's sexual orientation or gender identity will be when they are an adult. This seems reassuring to us playworkers in terms of supporting children to be who they want to be, how they want to be and how they want to play when they are in a play setting, as clearly the playing will enable them to experiment and get a sense of how it feels to be anybody or anything, while on neutral territory with no expectation of conformity to any of society's expectations. (Figure 9.1.)

In conversation, a ten-year-old Bea, when asked questions related to sex, gender and play at school, answers like this:

There is a group of girls who are like 'sporty', who sometimes play with some boys in the playground at school. There are girls who never do, and there are boys who aren't 'sporty', who never play with girls or the other boys. There's a big group of boys who play football, and no girls ever play with them when they are all together. We sometimes play 'Corners' with boys and girls. It's like a game of tag where you are on if not in a corner when tagged.

There is clearly a gender divide going on in this primary school playground, with some intermixing of boys and girls on limited occasions. Young children have 'an emotional investment in getting their gendered behaviour correct' (Martin 2011: 133) and as they grow, they do a lot of testing out gendered ideas in their playing. Thorne (1993) also talks of 'borderwork' where boys and girls sometimes come together, reducing the sense of difference but often strengthening the gender code of each group. Martin and Ruble (2010:366) say 'other children's sense of gender may emphasize avoiding gender-typical characteristics that they dislike: a girl may eschew the giggly, girly stuff; a boy may try to distance himself from macho elements of maleness'. However, when they look at gender segregation, they suggest that even when children are non-gender typical, generally they will still group themselves with other non-gender typical children of the same sex and identify with children of the same sex.

One day when I asked this boy if I could play football with them, he said, 'We don't play with ginger biscuits'. He had told me that he fancied my best friend but to keep it a secret, so I said to him, 'If you call me that again or be mean to me, I'll tell her that you fancy her'. That shut him up and he's been no trouble since. Ha-Ha! She doesn't like him and guess what? She's his Secret Santa. I wonder what she'll buy him.

These ten-year-olds have begun to play around with adolescent flirting play behaviour, which can consist of teasing, name-calling and so on. Maccoby (2003) gives examples of provocations that can occur, such as kiss chase; where if a girl catches a boy, she must kiss him to the delight of her girlfriends, but taunts from other boys. As children get older, cross-sex playing is often seen in more romantic or sexual terms and leads to teasing about fancying or loving the other child. This can sometimes be misinterpreted as bullying when it is perfectly natural play behaviour for children of this age. Bea responded to the taunt about not playing football by taunting in response.

There are no girls, in my year, who pretend to be boys, or boys who pretend to be girls, but there are 'tomboys' like, I suppose I'm one. We never wear dresses or skirts, and we don't giggle and be silly; we stand up for ourselves. I suppose having a brother might make a difference, but then my sister is like me too. She is fit, does dancing and stands up for herself, is brave, and is not girly, but we both like makeup and clothes and things as well. I suppose I sometimes wear skirts, but I'm still like sporty.

Bea differentiates between girly girls and tomboys or sporty girls. Girly girls giggle and wear dresses. Tomboys stand up for themselves and are brave, even if they like clothes and makeup. Halim et al. (2014) talk of how many girls, around the time they move to secondary schools, metamorphosize from girls who are girly into tomboys. Through their research, they consider that this may be due to a gathering realization that males are given greater regard than females. We wonder whether, in this decade – 2023, more adult males are taking to wearing and using clothes and skincare products previously considered feminine because of the strength of waves of feminism and the 'me too' agenda drawing more attention to the capabilities and strength of women; the greater awareness of transgender issues, or is it mainly the result of clever marketing? What do you think?

There are no couples who are going out or anything, although people develop crushes on other people. Like there's this girl who's a lesbian and she was going out with this girl who is a terrible attention-seeker. Anyway, we organized a wedding for them, and it was all underway when a group of boys came rushing in and spoilt everything. They've broken up since. The attention-seeker is now bisexual, of course. There's more drama in that.

Bea was very matter of fact about the lesbian couple and playing at weddings, but very disparaging about the attention-seeking girl deciding to be bisexual, suggesting that this was only a form of attention-seeking. This may have been just because the girl was already seen as being attention-seeking rather than because bisexuality was seen as something that would attract more attention than lesbianism. These children are only aged ten and eleven and as such, just exploring new ideas related to their sexual development, without necessarily having a full understanding of it. Waldner-Haugrud and MaGruder (1996) suggest from their research that girls were not as inhibited about expressing their same-gender preferences as boys because society was more flexible about girls not conforming to expected gendered behaviour. Young men feel greater pressure for gender differentiation Like gender contentedness, felt pressure for gender conformity is stronger for boys than girls' (Egan and Perry 2001): Researchers, such as Diamond (2000), are interested in how some adolescents depart from the socially constructed norms of gender and sexuality. She found that some girls, when faced with the option of choosing 'heterosexual', 'same sex attracted' or 'bisexual', preferred not to choose a label because their feelings do not fit into any of those categories. This is consistent with the idea of fluidity in some young women's sexuality during adolescence. This still seems to be the case today as it is suggested by a narrative in research on Gender and Sexual Identity in Adolescence, that those assigned female at birth, feel safer and more comfortable being flexible and fluid in their identity development process than those who are assigned male at birth (Hammack et al. 2022). It seems there is pressure on young men, from their peers, to demonstrate masculinity.

In most societies, there was, and to a great extent still is, an expectation that we will perform a gender role in public which is aligned with stereotyped views of how males and females should behave, at that time, within the local culture and that which is considered appropriate in the society in which we live. Often, this complies with heteronormative ideology, that is, that there are two separate genders and heterosexuality is a given. However, there are not only cultural views about what is considered suitable, as male and female behaviour, but also stereotyped ideas about male and female ability.

Both women and men have proved that in many areas of life, they have the same abilities, thus women now join the armed forces and become judges and men become househusbands and look after their children. In the West, schools curricula and Early Years provision are underpinned by these equalities. However, Wingrave (2014) discovered that, despite claims of gender blindness by early years practitioners in the UK, 'the data suggests that EYs, (early years settings) as do other areas of society, inculcate inherently gendered practices and attitudes' (ibid:156). What is your experience?

The Children's Society, Good Childhood Report (2020) suggests stereotyping of gender roles is alive and well, in that, of the young people interviewed, 44 per cent of girls against 32 per cent of boys considered being good-looking the most important aspect of their lives, and 1 in every 8 boys thought it is important to be tough. Ninety-five per cent of all the young people said they heard jokes or comments about other people's bodies and looks. When children were asked what attributes their friends would think were most important, after looking good it was that girls should be caring, and boys should be funny. So why is this? Geary (2019) suggests that although parents, other adults and cultural norms have influence over the way that children operate, when left to their own devices, children engage in activities and organize themselves in ways that are consistent with aspects of our evolutionary history. Do you believe this is true?

Looking at outcomes for children in LGBT parent families, based on research on parenting and child development in alternative families including lesbian mother families and gay father families, Golombok (2017:76) explains that 'The findings not only contest popular assumptions about the psychological consequences for children of being raised in new family forms but also challenge the supremacy of the traditional family'. This is borne out related to children with transgender parents too from research carried out by Penn State University (2022:1) that suggests that 'children with trans-gender parents play in ways that conform to gendered societal expectations, while others play in more gender-expansive ways'.

There are many different theories, developed and supported, about how and why boys and girls acquire their gender differences, and these can be roughly grouped into two main categories. Theories that have a socio-cultural, or external basis – gender differences caused by life experiences (Kohlberg 1966, Bem 1983, Thorne 1993, Rich-Harris 1999, Ding and Littleton 2005, Bandura and Walters 1963, Martin and Ruble 2004), and biological, or essentialist theories – gender differences caused by genetics, genes and hormones (Eliot 2010, Brizendine 2010, Gurian 2011, Sax 2005, Baron-Cohen 2004). Tenenbaum and Leaper (2002:626) suggest that upbringing affects what children consider is gender-appropriate for their sex, but children sort themselves out when it comes to playing and socializing. 'In other words, parents have an influence (though still modest) on what children think about what's "appropriate" for girls and boys, and not as much of an influence on how they actually play or engage with their friends'. Essentialists believe that there are certain characteristics that all males have and all females have (Sax 2005, Biddulph 1998, 2013). Biddulph (2013:19) says, 'Girls develop more quickly than boys, especially in brain ability'. This is caused by the oestrogen their body creates in the womb. He says that girls speak, write and draw earlier than boys and generally do not experience as much separation anxiety as boys. Do you think that beliefs about the causes of gender differences influence behaviour towards girls and boys?

Where has our evolutionary/social history got us in relation to gender roles, gender expression and gender identity? Young children will usually say 'I'm a girl' or 'I'm a boy' around two or three years old. However, The Children's Society research also revealed that some gender-diverse children start expressing their gender identity at the same time; becoming cross if they are called a girl when they feel like a boy or not wanting to wear the clothes that make them look as if they are a boy or girl. There are some parents who are now choosing not to reveal the sex of their babies and give them gender-neutral names, gender-neutral clothes and toys and so on, in the hope that the child will not grow up feeling pressured into behaving in certain gender stereotypical ways. What are your feelings about this?

A family has four children – two girls and two boys. However, one of the boys has identified as a girl since the age of about two, always wanting to wear girls' clothes, play with girls and their toys and be called a girl. 'Her' parents have gone along with this and have not put any pressure on the child to conform to gender-stereotyped expectations. They wait to see what the future may hold.

It may depend on whether the child has gender dysphoria (GD) – clinically significant distress or impairment related to a strong desire to be of another gender (American Psychiatric Association definition) or is Childhood Gender Non-conforming (CGN) which means the child does not conform to stereotyped expectations. The child has a brother and two sisters, and it may be that he identifies more with his sisters than with his brother. There are various reasons suggested as to why some older children may wish to transition such as sexuality confusion, mental health problems, neurodiversity, bullying and sexual harassment, abuse, hyper-sexualization of society and mental health problems. However, some children's physical sex just feels wrong to them.

Gentleman (2022) tells us that according to an NHS England Commissioned interim report, of the 5,000 referrals to Gender Identity Development Services (GIDS), about two-thirds of them were 'birth registered females first presenting in adolescence with gender-related distress'. The referrals had risen from 250, ten years ago, and at that time, the referrals were mainly boys. There is greatly increased publicity about children wanting to transition from one sex to another. In the past, most research was done on birth registered males, but as there is increased visibility in social media and acceptance with specific online and local support groups formed, it is easier for young people of both sexes to express a new trans identity.

The interim report suggests that parents and clinicians are trying to make sense of it, but there seems to be a lack of consensus within the medical profession about how to proceed as the long-term well-being of young people who have transitioned has not yet been fully assessed. Parents are anxious and uncertain about how to respond with conflicting advice from doctors and trans rights groups. Some parents are confused about the speed with which schools show a readiness to adopt a child's new identity. What are your feelings about this?

Elena's story

When I was in primary school, my friends (four other girls) used to play a game where we gave each other male versions of our names. So Linda became Luke, Ann became Andy, Brenda became Ben and Nancy became Nicholas. I (being Elena) was called Elliott; in fact, I was called Elliott Robert as my first and middle name (Rose) were changed to male versions.

In secondary school, I thought it would be fun to change my Facebook name to Elliott Robert instead of Elena Rose. My friends didn't like this and told me to change it back as they said it was confusing since this was now in the 'real' virtual world, not just a game we played among ourselves. However, I couldn't change it back as you can't change your name again on Facebook for thirty days, but I didn't mind that.

During secondary school, I started wondering about who I was and questioning things that I had taken for granted. I wondered about what it was and what it meant to be a girl, especially the expectations and assumptions people made about what it meant to be a girl or a boy. I started to play around with these ideas to explore them. I had my hair cut short and wore clothes designed as 'clothes for boys' or chose clothes that were neutral. I was exploring ideas about gender fluidity and gender binary. I remember being pleased that sometimes people thought I was a boy and sometimes people were not sure what I was, as I didn't like assumptions being made about me. I liked things being ambiguous.

I decided that I would like a more neutral sounding first name than Elena; I wondered about Oakley or Robyn. I asked my friends, and because I liked both names equally, I asked my friends to vote for which one I should use because I couldn't decide. They voted for Robyn. This is my preferred name, and I have changed it to this by deed poll, so it is officially my name. I kept Rose as my middle name because I liked it. Having played around with changing my names, I am now happy with my names.

Robyn, now aged nineteen, no longer dresses in an ambiguous way. She wears dresses and more fitted clothes rather than baggy, emphasizing her female figure. She says she is more content about who she is. She has a boyfriend. This gender outcome is very much in line with the idea that during puberty and teenage years, while trying to work themselves out, many children play around with their identity, and gender identity is one of the areas with which they can experiment. The outcome could have been different. Play helps with becoming.

Jacky was chatting with her friend and her friend's fourteen-year-old grandson. He said there were three people in his class who want to be known as 'they', not 'he' or 'she'. When asked how he felt about that, he said he didn't really care. It was up to them. None of them were his close friends, but they were OK. He didn't proffer whether they were originally she or he. The conversation continued with stories of children identifying as furries and, in one case a 'transparent toaster'. This caused much hilarity, and all three tried to decide what they would like to identify as. On reflection, Jacky wondered whether she should have been playing around with this with a fourteen-year-old. Could this lead to him thinking it was OK to disrespect other children's choices about identity? What are your thoughts on this?

Personal pronouns matter. They give people a 'sense of their place in the world but also for centuries have been used to keep them in their place, socially and politically' (Armistead 2022:2). It's a problem when a child wants their pronouns changed, in the same way as when a child wants to transition. People don't necessarily know how to respond and there does not seem to be a space for misgendering mistakes to be talked about without the 'perpetrator' being found guilty. In her article, Armistead (ibid) shares a quote, 'As a mother, wrestling with my child's pronouns can feel like being an explorer who has wandered off the edge of the map' and it can certainly be difficult to keep track of children's evolving and often very fierce demands to be referred to differently and to be differently gendered to society's previously accepted norms. It was clearly easier when such desires were not outwardly expressed and when children 'knew their place', in the same way that slaves and women were expected to know their place in the past. Happily, playworkers know their place – it is in service of children playing and thus if a child is playing with their gender identity, expression or personal pronoun, it is the playworker's job to support this, whatever the outcome may eventually be. Parents must understand this.

Perhaps one of the things this tells us is that children are quite accepting of their peers experimenting with their personas if it doesn't interfere with their own becoming and there is not too much drama made of it. *An older grandson told of a group of people in his class who made a big 'song and dance' about being called by the right pronoun and complained to the teachers if any of their fellow pupils got it wrong. However, one day, this same group of people were teasing a boy with autism about his behaviour, which incensed other classmates. They felt the group thought they had rights related to their gender identity but were not giving the boy with autism the same right to respect that they expected. They were accused of just being attention-seeking!* Attention-seeking seems to be something more undesirable than children playing around with their gender expression. Some children like the drama of being unlike others, and Apter (quoted in Armistead 2022) suggests that some requests to use 'they' are to gain special treatment – suggesting 'showing off'. What are your feelings about this?

A woman was giving an online presentation about children and play. As part of this, she explained that she was a feminist, and as such was horrified when her daughter bought her granddaughter a Barbie-like doll with long blond hair, an exaggerated female figure with all the usual girly accoutrements – high heels, a wardrobe of glamorous clothes and so on. However, after talking to the eight-year-old, she decided to trust the child to not be over-influenced to think that this was a 'normal' female. What the woman was delighted with was that left to her own devices to play with the doll in any way she wanted, led to all sorts of playing including making pretend money, designing and making beds for the tons of babies that the doll 'Bluey' adopted and having adventures.

Children sort themselves out when they play, and interference from adults to try and influence the play in any way, no matter how well-intentioned, is ruining the opportunity for a child to be real; to be themselves; to manage their own lives; and to experience wherever this takes them within their playing. 'Ultimately children are on their own journey, and we can support them and be a positive influence, but we cannot take the helm from them and control their course, and neither should we expect to do so' (Kilvington and Wood 2016:146). Do you agree with this?

Toys have become increasingly gendered over recent years, although there have been moves to try and correct this (Russell 2021). Many toy stores have pink sections for girls with mainly domestic toys such as cookery things, arts and crafts, and dolls with associated accoutrements, and blue sections, which are mainly wheeled and construction toys and superheroes – a clever marketing ploy on the part of toy makers and shops to sell more, sometimes the same things, for example, pink scooters for girls and blue scooters for boys. Most toddlers will play with anything, but as children get older, many of them may fall prey to this pressure from the media and their peers. However, as can be seen from the previous story and the following one, this does not necessarily mean that children will play in stereotypical ways with their stereotypical toys.

Lizzy (aged four) has many fairy-tale and Disney film character dolls, most of which are female. Most of these have that unreal look of Disney females, with perfect figures, large eyes, beautiful hair and many are dressed in wonderful dresses. Some of them, particularly the more modern female characters have storylines that describe them as strong, fearless and capable, but the older ones are usually in need of rescuing in their original stories. When they are new to her, Lizzy usually wants to play out some of the storylines as she's been read from a book or seen on a film, but after a while, the dolls are used as a whole variety of characters and in stories that she makes up herself.

On one occasion she played with six female dolls – two of them were husbands, two were wives, one was a maid and one was a friend/taxi-driver/witch/vet. Stories segued together seamlessly. First weddings were performed a few times (Lizzy had just been a flower girl at a wedding) and the taxi driver took the couples off in a taxi (basket) each time to go on honeymoons that involved mainly climbing mountains (up the back of the sofa); then the witch stole one of the husbands and the wife got him back after a fight with the witch; then a small soft toy lion and lizard were introduced. First, they kept stealing different characters and causing mayhem that was cleaned up by the superhero maid and eventually they became animals in a pet shop, along with a salt-cellar cat and a cushion owl, that were purchased, became ill and had to be seen by the vet. The stereotypically hyper-female gendered appearance of the dolls did not seem to feature in the playing at all.

Lizzy was an active agent in her own gender story. Lizzy has mainly played with boys during her early years and despite looking stereotypically girly with long hair, dressing in girly clothes and owning lots of girly toys, she loves to play at fighting, using tubes as weapons, climbing trees, setting traps, as well as playing in a more stereotypically girly way at house, drawing and colouring, dressing up herself and her dolls and so on. Her little brother often copies her, including putting on girly dressing-up clothes. He plays with stereotypically boys' toys and girls toys as well as gender-neutral toys. Their ages seem to be more relevant to how they play and what they play with, rather than their sex, but there are some things they love to do together such as whirling around and making themselves dizzy.

Ali, in our preface to Gender, Sex and Children's Play *(2016: xii)*, says, 'I had two older brothers, so it went without saying that I was a tomboy (although I don't like that word – it's another stereotypical label that doesn't fit). She says that she 'refused to fit neatly into the "girl box" but leapt in and out of it *throughout childhood'*. Do you think that having male and female siblings or friends in the early years makes a difference to the way that children express their gender and play?

What are your views on stereotypical toys for girls and boys – should they be avoided? Do you think the toys that children play with influence the way they view themselves and how they develop in later life? Play and child development specialist Gummer (quoted in Barford 2014) thinks a healthy play diet is important so that children have choices across the spectrum. Many play settings provide loose parts such as sand, water, sticks, pebbles, tyres, boxes, cloths and so on, and these have no gender attachments. We are not aware of any research that looks at whether playing with loose parts influences later gender development.

Elwood (2021) tells us in her PsyPost that a longitudinal study on engagement with princess culture in preschool and later gender stereotypical behaviour, carried out by Coyne et al. (2021), concluded in unexpected results. 'Surprisingly, princess culture during the preschool years was not tied to later engagement in female gender-stereotyped behavior. Rather, princess culture appeared to have an overall positive impact on children's gender development' (Elwood 2021:2) and this included boys and girls. Is this another example of overanxious adults assuming that children have no agency of their own? In his article about toy guns, De Koven (2016:1) suggests that parents don't trust kids and they don't trust play. He says that 'The stuff of kids play is reality. Safe in the fiction of the game, kids can deal with the truth of their world, even though their parents are in denial'. There is no firm evidence from any piece of research that playing with toy guns as a child is associated with the development of future use of real guns.

Ollie, an eleven-year-old boy, says that his school has some strict guidelines about things that should and shouldn't be said, some related to gender. For example, children should call each other by name and not as boys or girls; they should not compliment other children on their appearance as it could be seen as sexist; if someone wants to be called 'they' or changes their name to something non-gendered, they should not tease or question them about it; they should not exclude anyone from playing on the strength of their sex or suggest that boys or girls are better at different things.

As a postscript to this, Ollie has moved to his secondary school, and three of his friends now have 'girlfriends'. According to his mother, all the boys and girls are very kind to each other and there is no taunting about the relationships. Ollie's girlfriend clearly likes everything about him, as evidenced by a letter she sent her best friend that was forwarded to Ollie.

This is a very well-meaning attempt to regulate the behaviour of school children by issuing rules and holding mixed-sex activities. However, in a play situation, there are no such rules or regulations; children sort themselves out. When asked about it, Ollie said he thought it was a good idea to have the rules, but a bit silly, and that despite the rules, the boys played football together and the girls played together. This is very consistent with Martin, Fabes and Hanish's (2014) views related to gender in educational contexts. But it seems that as children mature, this powerful gender segregation changes.

> In summary, gender segregation is a pervasive and powerful social phenomenon. Children learn about the 'culture' of their gender group from spending time with same-sex peers: that is, they learn how members of their sex communicate, the activities they like, and the ways they behave. (Priess and Shibley Hyde 2011:1)

Many of us will have seen groups of young teenagers 'hanging out' in mixed-sex groups in parks, on street corners, coming out of school and at bus stops. Priess and Shibley Hyde (2011:1) tell us that 'Single-gender peer groups prior to adolescence give way to cliques that are increasingly composed of both genders across the teenage years', and these cliques are sometimes the basis of early sexual relationships. Thorne and Luria (1986:187) suggest that the 'gender-marked rituals of teasing, chasing, and pollution heighten the boundaries between boys and girls' in elementary school and as they go into adolescence this is the basis upon which early relationships develop. They argue that because children's sexual knowledge is fragmentary and distinctly different from that of adults, scripting in same-gender peer groups may be more about gender than sexual orientation. In this sense, at this age, children are learning about masculinity and femininity rather than sexuality per se, although heterosexuality is embedded within these concepts.

Do boys, girls and transgender children play in gendered ways? Kilvington and Wood (2016) discovered that, no matter how many different pieces of research from a wide range of disciplines were studied, and no matter what the implications are, the overall conclusion was that 'play behaviours are generally observed to be the largest form of difference between girls and boys' (ibid:81). The reasons posited for this were many and varied, yet none appeared to be conclusive. It also seems that meta-analyses of gender-related differences in children's toy preferences found that gender differences and gender-specific effects on children's toy preferences are large and reliable, and that some toys that researchers have classified as neutral may actually be preferred by girls (Davis and Hines 2020). We wonder if this difference is equally obvious in transgender children.

From their research with 317 transgender, 316 cisgender children and 189 siblings, aged three to twelve years old, Gulgoz et al. (2018) found that the young children who had identified, from a young age, as a different sex to the one that they were assigned with at birth (transgender), show gender development in line with the development of young children who have always identified with their assigned sex (cisgender). For example, their play patterns are stereotypical within the sex they identify with, and not their assigned sex. This includes across a spectrum of girly girls, tomboys, macho boys, cissy boys and so on, that is, a transgender girl may still enjoy climbing trees and playing with construction toys, in line with being a tomboy while identifying as a girl. This pattern was demonstrated regardless of how long the child had lived as their assigned sex. Their 'findings suggest that early sex assignment and parental rearing based on that sex assignment do not always define how a child identifies or expresses gender later' (ibid:24480). Interestingly, this research suggests the strong role of self-socialization processes on the development of gender identity – not peer, society or parental pressure and socialization or biological tendency. This is very much in line with the playwork idea of children being agents in their own lives and not just prey to the whims of their biological inheritance or adult pressure. 'This coherence suggests a powerful role of individuals' views of themselves and of self-socialization processes on the development of gender typing' (ibid).

Regardless of how or why children develop their gender identities and how genderized the play of the children who attend our settings is, as people who work with children – playworkers, teachers, early years workers, paediatric medical staff, children's social workers, therapists, sports coaches and so on – we have a professional duty to work within an equal opportunities policy, including in relation to sex, gender and sexual orientation. These policies will vary in precise wording between settings but in practice will have at their root the obligation for adults to treat children fairly and not to disadvantage any of them because of a particular aspect of their being. Sometimes we can be unaware of our biases and how we might be disadvantaging, for instance, children who are confused about their gender identity, by the language we use, the resources we offer, the way we respond to their appearance or concerns and the regard given to some aspects of our attendees and the setting and not others. Playworkers respond to different children differently, according to their perceived individual need.

There are several ways in which we and play settings can check our own behaviour and the environment in relation to sex and gender equality through reflexive reflection, team reflection, auditing and regular updating. The Scottish Care Inspectorate (2018) published a guide for gender-equal play in early learning and care, giving suggestions such as:

- Look at your surroundings and do a 'gender' audit of your play area.
- Are certain areas of the room (outside space) favoured by one gender in particular?
- Think about how you organize the space.
- What are some of my own biases, values and belief systems in relation to gender?
- How might these gender values/beliefs influence the way I interact with children?
- Do I engage differently with boys and girls?

The more gender-neutral loose parts, games, equipment, toys, dressing-up clothes and so on are in a play setting, the fairer will be the offering to children, whatever their current or becoming sex, gender identity, or sexuality. Natural outdoor settings offer only gender-neutral affordances. Girls and boys may, or may not, play differently with the possibilities, but trees, bushes, grass, earth, sand, water, pebbles, rocks, flowers, sticks, wind, rain and so on have no gender significance built into them. Have you noticed the different sexes playing differently with natural elements outside?

There seems to be some researched differences in the way that children participate in the outdoors, although much of this has been associated with levels of physical activity in the outdoors rather than interaction with natural objects. For example, Reimers, Schoeppe and Knapp (2018:1) found 'Girls' physical activity seems to be suppressed in the presence of boys' in public playgrounds in Germany. Brockman, Jago and Fox (2011:1) interviewed seventy children in Bristol, aged ten and eleven and reported that 'children's activities during active play (this involved outdoor active play) varied by gender'. Girls played outside in the garden, with family, friends or pets. Boys were reported as generally doing specific activities such as riding bikes and playing ball further from home.

Vaughn (2013) in *The Guardian* describes RSPB research on 1,200 children's affinity with nature. Here is one observation of both boys and girls playing: *Two young boys are putting the finishing touches to their twig-lined den, next to a welly-clad girl who has discovered a toad hiding by a tree. Several children are busy fishing for worms, while others are scooping up bird feathers as part of their treasure hunt*. From their findings, they conclude that girls have a better connection with nature than boys.

Flannigan and Dietze (2018), in their research on outdoor play, children and loose parts in the early years, notice that boys and girls played with similar things and in similar ways, engaging in the same sorts of activities when playing outside and with loose parts. Boys and girls engaged in good versus bad themes and rough and tumble play. Both boys and girls also engaged in house and family themes and 'at no time did the children verbalize to their peers that they could not play due to their gender' (ibid:57/8). It was concluded that 'natural outdoor environment and the provision of gender-neutral loose parts supported gender-inclusive and equitable play' (ibid:58).

This leaves us with what should playworkers make of all this? While acknowledging that our world has moved on since 2016, we return to the suggestions made in the Afterword of Kilvington and Wood (2016:145–9), as they are still relevant in 2023.

- Children 'need opportunities and freedom to discover and express their human identity' (ibid:146) in all its aspects and during play is the perfect time for them to experiment with this.
- We need to understand ourselves – our own gender and sexuality journey and where it has led us to and how it affects our views.
- We need to be aware of our own gendered and non-gendered behaviour and use of language and how we respond to girls, boys and others. Might there be a difference, and might we be role-modelling things we are unaware of? Are we comfortable with trans children and altered personal pronouns, and if not, how can we change?
- Children are young at a different time than when we were young, and their world is different. The world is ever changing. Trying to see it through their eyes requires a mind-shift. We must work at being able to 'see things from their changing perspectives' (ibid:147) and this requires work on our part. Children 'cannot see the world through an adult lens' (ibid) but we can work at trying to see through theirs.
- If we 'unobtrusively observe and listen to children playing' (ibid), without interfering, we will learn much about them and their perspectives. Many adults find this almost impossible. It is worth working at as we adults have much to learn.
- We must think about the provision of resources; the creation of spaces and the opportunities for play, to check for gender biases; to increase provision of non-gendered spaces and loose parts; lessen the numbers

of obviously stereotypically gendered toys, books and areas; increase the numbers of non-gendered toys, books and areas so that all children, whatever their sex, gender identity or sexuality at the time, have a 'rich and diverse play diet' (ibid:148).
- Believe and trust in children's agency, their competence and capability. Playing gives children whole worlds of possibility. 'Ultimately children are on their own journey, and we can support them and be a positive influence, but we cannot take the helm from them and control their course, and neither should we expect to do so' (ibid:146).

Afterword

We hope that in this book we have helped to further develop ideas about play and playwork practice that may be used not only by playworkers but also across the children's workforce and in everyday life. If we return to Brown, Long and Wragg's (2018) summary of what guides playwork practice, we have included and extended, throughout the book, information about and/or examples of all of the characteristics mentioned that make the playwork approach one that supports children no matter what the context for playing. These characteristics are, in summary, the following:

- flattening the usual hierarchy of adults being in charge;
- children playing for no purpose other than being in the moment;
- the less involvement by adults, the better the vital outcomes that come from playing;
- an unconditional regard for children as they really are and not as idealized versions of children;
- a willingness to relinquish all adult power and preconceptions so the power rests with the children;
- the provision of flexible environments that can be altered in many ways by children to suit their own ideas;
- the benefits of risky play and the need for considered intervention only if there is a safety or safeguarding issue involved;
- an ongoing commitment to reflexive reflection, looking at how our own child-self may affect our adult self and therefore the way we work with children.

Penny Wilson rather splendidly talks about 'play literacy' which also underpins the philosophy behind playwork practice.

> Play Literacy is our ability to read, interpret, sense and understand the essence of play; an ability to communicate in a common language about play. It is a set of skills and knowledge needed to recognise play, know when to interact and intervene and how to avoid interference. It is the ability to evaluate and analyse play in order to provide credible and meaningful information about it to others and to be able to design and sustain an environment in which play

is given time, space and validation. It is also recognising that the essence of play can and should be found in everyday experiences. (Wilson 2020)

We hope we have given you enough 'credible and meaningful' information about playwork practice that will enable you to understand the importance of protecting children's right to have time to play without interference, and without pressure of expectation, from us well-meaning adults. We wish you well in your own journey – wherever you live and work – in observing and supporting children's self-directed play and learning all they can teach us, for they are the experts.

Appendix

Appendix 1

Playwork Principles

These principles establish the professional and ethical framework for playwork and as such must be regarded as a whole.

They describe what is unique about play and playwork and provide the playwork perspective for working with children and young people.

They are based on the recognition that children and young people's capacity for positive development will be enhanced if given access to the broadest range of environments and play opportunities.

1. All children and young people need to play. The impulse to play is innate. Play is a biological, psychological and social necessity, and is fundamental to the healthy development and well-being of individuals and communities.
2. Play is a process that is freely chosen, personally directed and intrinsically motivated. That is, children and young people determine and control the content and intent of their play by following their own instincts, ideas and interests, in their own way for their own reasons.
3. The prime focus and essence of playwork is to support and facilitate the play process, and this should inform the development of play policy, strategy, training and education.
4. For playworkers, the play process takes precedence, and playworkers act as advocates for play when engaging with adult-led agendas.
5. The role of the playworker is to support all children and young people in the creation of a space in which they can play.
6. The playworker's response to children and young people playing is based on a sound, up-to-date knowledge of the play process and reflective practice.

7. Playworkers recognize their own impact on the play space and also the impact of children and young people's play on the playworker.
8. Playworkers choose an intervention style that enables children and young people to extend their play. All playworker interventions must balance risk with the developmental benefit and well-being of children.

Playwork Principles Scrutiny Group (2005), *The Playwork Principles*, Cardiff: Play Wales.

Appendix 2

Play Types

Symbolic play

Play which allows control, gradual exploration and increased understanding without being out of one's depth, by using symbols, that is, objects, designs or signs to represent people, ideas or qualities. For example, using a piece of wood to symbolize a person or a weapon, a piece of string to symbolize a wedding ring, a length of rope to symbolize a boundary, a carrot to symbolize a microphone, building a shrine, creating a flag.

Exploratory play (finding out play)

Play to access factual information about an environment and engaging with the area or thing and, by either manipulation or movement, assessing its properties, possibilities and content. For example, stacking bricks, taking a camera apart, digging 'to Australia'.

Object play (problem-solving play)

Play which uses infinite and interesting sequences of hand-eye manipulations and movements. For example, examination and novel use of any object, for example, cloth, rope, bubble wrap, paintbrush, cup. The fascination here is with the object itself and what it can do or be (regardless of what its 'proper use' might be).

Rough and tumble play

Close encounter play which is less to do with fighting and more to do with touching, tickling, gauging relative strength, discovering physical flexibility and the exhilaration of display. Finding out and testing one's own and other's limits. Learning social and interpersonal codes of physical conduct. For example, playful fighting, wrestling and chasing where the children are obviously unhurt and giving every indication that they are enjoying themselves.

Socio-dramatic play

The enactment of real and potential experiences of an intense personal, social, domestic or interpersonal nature, that is, re-creating scenes from own life. For example, playing at house, going to the shops, being mums and dads, organizing a meal, having a row, funerals, divorce courts. Sometimes acting out emotions too scary to express in real life – often therapeutic.

Dramatic play

Play which dramatizes events in which the child is not a direct participator, that is, re-creating scenes from others' lives or from telly or theatre. For example, presentation of a TV show, an event on the street or in the news, a religious or festive event, a birth or death, or being famous footballers or a band in a recent match or concert. Sometimes done for an audience.

Social play

Play during which the rules and criteria for social engagement, interaction and communication can be revealed, explored and amended. Any social or interactive situation which contains an expectation on all parties that they will discuss and abide by certain rules, customs or protocols, for example, games, conversations, making something together, challenging, discussing.

Communication play

Play using words, nuances or gestures, for example, mime, jokes, play-acting, mickey taking, singing, debate, poetry, graffiti, swearing, making up languages/words/slang, storytelling. Creating a reaction and exploring the impact.

Creative play (inventive play)

Play which allows a new response, an expression of self, the transformation of information, awareness of new connections and new insights, with an element of surprise. It is about focused but spontaneous creation with a wide range of materials and tools for its own sake, with real freedom and not necessarily an end result. Could be small or large scale, individual or group.

Deep play

Play which allows the child to encounter risky or even potentially life-threatening experiences to develop survival skills and conquer fear. For example, leaping onto an aerial runway, riding a bike on a parapet, balancing on a high beam. The risk will be from the child's perspective (certainly not the adults') and so the same experience could be deep play for one child and not the other.

Fantasy play

Play which rearranges the world in the child's way, a way which is complete fantasy and unreal, for example, being superheroes, aliens, goblins, timelords, flying a UFO, casting spells, saving the world from certain destruction.

Imaginative play

Play where the conventional rules that govern the physical world do not apply but is still based on reality. For example, imagining you are, or pretending to be, a tree, a ship or an animal, patting a dog which isn't there, having an invisible friend, imagining a table is a bus or a cave.

Role-play

Play exploring identity and ways of being and doing, although not normally of an intense personal, social, domestic or interpersonal nature. Often imitating someone or trying out something seen but not experienced, for example, driving a car, playing dead, being a clown or a shopkeeper ...

Locomotor play

Movement in any and every direction – up, down, along, at various speeds and seemingly for its own sake. For example, chasing, tagging, hiding and seeking, tree climbing, rolling, jumping, dancing. Experiencing the possibilities of one's body within a particular environment. This includes ranging.

Mastery play

Generally expressed by taking (and feeling) control of the physical and affective ingredients of the natural environment. For example, digging holes and tunnels in earth or sand, changing the course of streams, constructing shelters, building fires. However, it could also include mastering a new skill, for example, a jump across a river, or riding a bike.

Recapitulative play

Play that displays aspects of human evolutionary history, stored and passed on through our genes and manifested when children play spontaneously – often stimulated by aspects of the outdoor environment like forests and shallow pools/rivers. For example, lighting fires, engaging in spontaneous rituals and songs, dressing up in historic clothes/uniforms and role-playing, playing wars and making weapons, growing and cooking things, creating ancient style communities, building shelters, creating languages and religions.

Adapted from Hughes, B. (2002), *A Playworker's Taxonomy of Play Types*, 2nd edn, London: PlayLink.

Appendix 3

Risk/Benefit Assessment Form

Risk/Benefit Assessment Form

Likelihood: 1-no harm 2 harm happens rarely 3-harm happens occasionally 4-harm happens sometimes 5-harm happens regularly 6-harm every time children do this
Severity: 1 - minor cuts & grazes 2 - cuts, sprains 3 - head injury/hospital visit 4 - significant injury or paralysis 5 -death 6- multiple deaths

		Severity					
Likelihood		1	2	3	4	5	6
	6	6	12	18	24	30	36
	5	5	10	15	20	25	30
	4	4	8	12	16	20	24
	3	3	6	9	12	15	18
	2	2	4	6	8	10	12
	1	1	2	3	4	5	6

Location: ......Primary School	Date: 07/06/23	Risk Assessment undertaken by: Lunchtime staff in agreement with Head Teacher	Signed:

a	b	c	d	e	f	g	h
What is being risk assessed? (i.e. environment/ play opportunity/ activity/ event, location, group size & ratio, other. Eg. climbing a tree,	What is/are the likely injury/problem etc	Likelihood of it happening 1-6	Severity of injury 1-6	Risk level (c×d=e)	What is the value/benefit of the play opportunity etc to the children/young people?	Measures taken to eliminate/reduce the hazard to an acceptable level of risk	Date of next review
Play fighting	Children engaging in play fighting (with our without scrap/loose parts) may get hit over the head, on the face or on the body – this may result in grazes, bumps, bruises, scratches and/or mild concussion	2	1-2	2-4 LOW	As with all mammals, rough & tumble play is an important part of children's development. Some children (esp. boys) have an innate desire to engage in this kind of play Physical exercise Agility Learning about social rules Learning control & boundaries Emotion regulation Emotional resilience Learning what they can give and what they can take Engaging in fantasy play 'Playing out' situations in a safe & emotionally secure environment Building relationships It's enjoyable	*Talk to children about what measures they could put in place to make it safe without losing beneficial risk & fun eg. ensuring sufficient space *Introduce a scrap on scrap rule to avoid hitting bodies *Decide on appropriate scrap for play fighting ie cardboard tubes and foam sticks, not guttering or plastic pipes *Lunchtime staff trained to monitor and undertake dynamic risk benefit assessment *Communicate 'rules' and measures with all staff and children	

Note: Columns *c* & *d* should be expressed on a scale of *1 – 6*. To assess the risk level, multiply the figure in column *c* by that in column *d*. The resulting score (risk level) is entered into column *e*. **1-12 = Low risk, 13-24 = Medium risk, 24-36 = High risk.**

Figure A3.1 Risk/Benefit Assessment Form.

References

Ackerman, D. (1999), *Deep Play*, New York: Vintage Books.

Ainscow, M., T. Booth and A. Dyson (2006), 'Inclusion and the standards agenda: Negotiating policy pressures in England', *International Journal of Inclusive Education*, 10(4–5): 295–308. Available online: https://doi.org/10.1080/13603110500430633 (accessed 1 March 2023).

Alexander, S.A., K.L. Frohlich and C. Fusco (2014), 'Playing for health? Revisiting health promotion to examine the emerging public health position on children's play', *Health Promotion International*, 29(1): 155–64. Available online: https://doi.org/10.1093/heapro/das042 (accessed 20 November 2022).

Allen of Hurtwood, Lady Marjory. (1968), *Planning for Play*, London: Thames and Hudson.

Anderson, B. (2014), *Encountering Affect: Capacities, Apparatuses, Conditions*, Farnham: Ashgate Publishing Company.

Andrews, M. (2012), *Exploring Play for Early Childhood Studies*, London: Sage.

Appleton, M. (2002), *Summerhill – A Free Range Childhood*, Loughton: Gale Centre Publications.

Ardelean, A., K. Smith and W. Russell (2021), *The Case for Play in Schools: A Review of the Literature*, Bristol: OPAL.

Argyris, C. and D. Schon (1974), *Theory in Practice: Increasing Professional Effectiveness*, San Francisco: Jossey-Bass.

Armistead, C. (2022), 'It's complicated – But you can't shy away from it': Everything you wanted to know about pronouns (but were afraid to ask)', *The Guardian*, 26 November. Available online: https://www.theguardian.com/world/2022/nov/26/pronouns-gendered-language-revolution-britain (accessed 1 March 2023).

Aumann, K. and A. Hart (2009), *Helping Children with Complex Needs Bounce Back: Resilient Therapy for Parents and Professionals*, London: Jessica Kingsley Publishers.

Axline, V. (1947), *Play Therapy*, Ballantine Books.

Baines, E. and P. Blatchford (2019), *School Break and Lunch Times and Young People's Social Lives: A Follow-Up National Study*, London: Department of Psych & Human Development UCL Institute of Education.

Ball, D., T. Gill and B. Spiegel (2012), *Managing Risk in Playwork Provision: Implementation Guide*, 2nd edn, London: National Children's Bureau.

References

Ball-King, L. (2021), 'Benefit-risk assessment: Balancing the benefits and risks of leisure', *World Leisure Journal*, 64(4): 383–98. Available online: https://doi.org/10.1080/16078055.2022.2052952 (accessed 25 February 2023).

Bandura, A. and R.H. Walters (1963), *Social Learning and Personality Development*, New York: Holt Rinehart and Winston.

Barad, K. (2007), *Meeting the Universe Halfway*, Durham, NC: Duke University Press.

Barclay, M. and B. Tawil (2022a), 'Part 2_risk and play: A balanced approach', *Ludicology*, 27 April. Available online: https://ludicology.com/store-room/risk-and-play-a-balanced-approach (accessed 25 February 2023).

Barclay, M. and B. Tawil (2022b), 'Part 1_Take a risk on play', *Ludicology*, 27 April. Available online: https://ludicology.com/store-room/take-a-risk-on-play (accessed 25 February 2023).

Barford, V. (2014), 'Do children's toys influence their career choices?' *BBC News Magazine*, 27 January. Available online: https://www.bbc.co.uk/news/magazine-25857895 (accessed 1 March 2023).

Barnado's. (2020), 'Time for a clean slate; Children's mental health at the heart of education', *Barnardo's*, May. Available online: https://www.barnardos.org.uk/sites/default/files/uploads/time-for-clean-slate-mental-health-at-heart-education-report.pdf (accessed 25 February 2023).

Baron-Cohen, S. (2004), *Essential Differences: Male and Female Brains and the Truth About Autism*, New York: Basic Books.

Beames, S. and M. Brown (2016), *Adventurous Learning: A Pedagogy for a Changing World*, London: Routledge.

Bekoff, M. (2007), *Animals Matter: A Biologist Explains Why We Should Treat Animals with Compassion and Respect*, Boston, MA: Shambhala Publications.

Bem, S.L. (1983), 'Gender schema theory and its implications for child development: Raising gender-aschematic children in a gender-schematic society', *Signs: Journal of Women in Culture and Society*, 8(4): 598–616. Available online: https://www.jstor.org/stable/3173685 (accessed 25 March 2023).

Besag, V. (2002), 'The playground', in M. Elliot (ed), *Bullying - A Practical Guide to Coping for Schools*, 3rd edn, 195–206, London: Pearson Education in conjunction with Kidscape.

Beunderman, J. (2010), *People Make Play – The Impact of Staffed Play Provision on Children, Families and Communities*, London: National Children's Bureau.

Biddulph, S. (1998), *Raising Boys: Why Boys Are Different and How to Help Them Become Happy Well-Balanced Men*, London: Thomsons.

Biddulph, S. (2013), *Raising Girls*, London: Harper Thornsons.

Blaxter, M. (2010), *Health*, 2nd edn, Cambridge: Polity.

Blundell, D. (2016), *Rethinking Children's Spaces and Places*, London: Bloomsbury.

Bolton, G. (2010), *Reflective Practice: Writing and Professional Development*, 3rd Ed., London: Sage Publishing.

Borkett, P. (2018), *Cultural Diversity and Inclusion in Early Years Education*, Abingdon: Routledge.

Bozalek, V. and S. Fullagar (2022), 'Able/disabled', in K. Murris (ed), *A Glossary for Doing Postqualitative, New Materialist and Critical Posthumanist Research Across Disciplines*, 2–3, London: Routledge.

Briggs, M. and A. Hansen (2012), *Play-Based Learning in the Primary School*, London: Sage.

Brizendine, I. (2010), *The Male Brain*, New York: Broadway Books.

Brock, A. (2019), 'Perspective 2: Capitalising on play – Harnessing it for learning', in A. Brock, P. Jarvis and Y. Olusoga (eds), *Perspectives on Play: Learning for Life*, 3rd edn, 17–30, London: Routledge.

Brock, A., P. Jarvis and Y. Olusoga, eds (2019), *Perspectives on Play: Learning for Life*, 3rd edn, Abingdon: Routledge.

Brock, A., S. Dodds, P. Jarvis and Y. Olusoga, eds (2009), *Perspectives on Play: Learning for Life*, Harlow: Pearson Longman.

Brockman, R., R. Jago and K. Fox (2011), 'Children's active play: Self-reported motivators, barriers and facilitators', *BMC Public Health*, 11(461). Available online: https://research.childrenandnature.org/research/girls-and-boys-active-play-outdoors-differs-in-terms-of-activities-location-and-social-context/ (accessed 1 March 2023).

Brown, F. (2003), 'Compound flexibility: The role of playwork in child development', in F. Brown (ed), *Playwork: Theory and Practice*, 51–65, Buckingham: Open University Press.

Brown, F. (2008), 'The fundamentals of playwork', in F. Brown and C. Taylor (eds), *Foundations of Playwork*, 7–13, Maidenhead: McGraw-Hill, Open University Press.

Brown, F. (2013), *Play Deprivation: Impact, Consequences and the Potential of Playwork*, Wales: Play Wales.

Brown, F. (2014), *Play and Playwork - 101 Stories of Playing*, Maidenhead: Open University Press.

Brown, F. (2015), 'The principles of playwork', in J.E. Johnson, S.G. Eberle, T.S. Henricks and D.S. Kuschner (eds), *The Handbook of the Study of Play*, 406–22, London: Rowman & Littlefield.

Brown, F. and B. Cheeseman (2003), 'Introduction: Childhood and play', In F. Brown (ed), *Playwork Theory and Practice*, 1–6, Open University Press.

Brown, F., A. Long and M. Wragg (2018), 'Playwork: A unique way of working with children', in P.K. Smith and J. Roopnarine (eds), *The Cambridge*

Handbook of Play: Developmental and Disciplinary Perspectives, 704–21, Cambridge: Cambridge University Press.

Brown, S. (2009), *Play – How It Shapes the Brain, Opens the Imagination and Invigorates the Soul*, London: Avery.

Bruce, T. (2011a), *Early Childhood Education*, 4th edn, London: Hodder Education.

Bruce, T. (2011b), *Learning Through Play: For Babies, Toddlers and Young Children*, 2nd edn, Abingdon: Hodder Education.

Bruner, J.S. (1966), *Towards a Theory of Instruction*, Cambridge: Harvard University Press.

Brussoni, M., L.L. Olsen, I. Pike and D.A. Sleet (2012), 'Risky play and children's safety: Balancing priorities for optimal child development', *International Journal of Environmental Research and Public Health*, 9(9): 3134–48. Available online: https://doi.org/10.3390/ijerph9093134 (accessed 25 March 2023).

Bryan, J. (2012), *From the Dress-up Corner to the Senior Prom: Navigating Gender and Sexuality Diversity in Prek-12 Schools*, Lanham: Rowman & Littlefield Education.

Burghardt, G.M. (2005), *The Genesis of Animal Play Testing the Limits*, Cambridge: MIT Press.

Burnett, C. and G. Merchant (2016), 'Assembling virtual play in the classroom', in B. Parry, C. Burnett, and G. Merchant (eds), *Literacy, Media, Technology Past, Present and Future*, 219–32, London: Bloomsbury.

Callios, R. ([1961] 2001), *Man, Play and Games*, Chicago: University of Illinois Press.

Campbell, F.K. (2009), *Contours of Ableism*, Basingstoke: Palgrave Macmillan.

Care Inspectorate. (2018), *Gender Equal Play; in Early Learning and Childcare*, Scotland, Care Inspectorate Communications. Available online: https://hub.careinspectorate.com/media/3466/gender-equal-play-in-early-learning-and-childcare.pdf (accessed 1 March 2023).

Cattanach, A. (1994), *Play Therapy – Where the Sky Meets the Underworld*, London: Jessica Kingsley Publishers.

Cattanach, A. (2008), *Play Therapy with Abused Children*, 2nd edn, London: Jessica Kingsley Publisher.

Centre for Mental Health. (2014), 'Childhood behavioural problems – A briefing for child social workers'. Available online: https://www.centreformentalhealth.org.uk/sites/default/files/2018-09/socialworkers.pdf (accessed 27 February 2023).

Chaarani, B., J. Ortigara, D. Yuan, H. Loso, A. Potter and H.P. Garavan (2022), 'Association of video gaming with cognitive performance among children', *Jama Network Open*, 5(10): e2235721. Available online: https://jamanetwork.com/journals/jamanetworkopen/fullarticle/2797596 (accessed 25 February 2023).

Chinn, D. (2007), 'Reflection and reflexivity', *Clinical Psychology Forum*, 1(178): 13–16. Available online: https://www.researchgate.net/publication/292453531_Reflection_and_reflexivity (accessed 1 June 2022).

Claparede, E. (1928), 'Feelings and emotions', in M.L. Reymert (ed), *Feelings and Emotions: The Wittenberg Symposium*, 124–39, Worcester: Clarke University Press.

Clifton, G. (2014), 'In conversation with… Zoë readhead, principal of summerhill school, Leiston, Suffolk', *Journal of Pedagogic Development*, 4(2): 33–41. Available online: https://www.beds.ac.uk/media/244697/in-conversation-with-zoe-readhead-principal-of-summerhill-school-leiston-suffolk.pdf. (accessed 25 February 2023).

Conway, M. (2009), 'Developing an adventure playground: The essential elements', *Practice Briefing 1*, London: NCB.

Coyne, S.M., J.R. Linder, M. Booth, S. Keenan-Kroff, J.E. Shawcroft and C. Yang (2021), 'Princess power: Longitudinal associations between engagement with princess culture in preschool and gender stereotypical behavior, body esteem, and hegemonic masculinity in early adolescence', *Child Development*, 92(6): 2413–30. Available online: https://doi.org/10.1111/cdev.13633 (accessed 1 March 2023).

Crowe, B. (1983), *Play Is a Feeling*, London: George, Allen & Unwin.

Cullen, F. and C. Johnston (2018), 'Playwork goes to school: Professional (mis) recognition and playwork practice in primary school', *Pedagogy, Culture and Society*, 26(3): 467–84. Available online: https://doi.org/10.1080/14681366.2017.1421569 (accessed 25 February 2023).

Damasio, A. (1999), *The Feeling of What Happens: Body and Emotion in the Making of Consciousness*, London: Harcourt, Brace & Co.

Damasio, A. (2003), *Looking for Spinoza: Joy, Sorrow, and the Feeling Brain*, London: Houghton Mifflin Harcourt.

Darwin, C.R. (1872), *The Expression of the Emotions in Man and Animals*, London: John Murray.

Davie, M. and M. Butler (2017), 'Behavioural issues in children', *Paediatric FOAMed*. Available online: https://www.paediatricfoam.com/2017/07/behavioural-issues-in-children/ (accessed 27 February 2023).

Davis, J.T.M. and M. Hines (2020), 'How large are gender differences in toy preferences? A systematic review and meta-analysis of toy preference research', *Archives of Sexual Behavior*, 49(2): 373–94. Available online: https://doi.org/10.1007/s10508-019-01624-7(accessed 28 February 2023).

De Koven, B.L. (2016), 'Toys guns are toys guns bad for kid? Or for adults?' *Psychology Today*, January 20. Available online: https://www.psychologytoday.com/gb/blog/having-fun/201601/toy-guns (accessed 1 March 2023).

Dégi, Z. and A. Asztalos (2021), 'Scouts' and educational stakeholders' perceptions of integrating scouting methods into formal education', *Central

European Journal of Educational Research, 3(2): 98–109. Available online: https://doi.org/10.37441/cejer/2021/3/2/9365 (accessed 1 March 2023).

Deleuze, G. and F. Guattari (1987), *A Thousand Plateaus. Capitalism and Schizophrenia*, Minneapolis: University of Minnesota Press.

Delorme, M. (2018), 'Hysterical about playwork', in F. Brown and B. Hughes (eds), *Aspects of Playwork: Play and Culture Studies*, 179–91, Lanham: Rowman & Littlefield.

Department for Education. (2013), 'Behaviour and discipline in schools – advice for headteachers and school staff', February 2014. Available online: https://assets.publishing.service.gov.uk/government/uploads/system/uploads/attachment_data/file/353921/Behaviour_and_Discipline_in_Schools_-_A_guide_for_headteachers_and_school_staff.pdf (accessed 28 February 2023).

Diamond, L. (2000), 'Sexual identity, attractions, and behavior among young sexual-minority women over a two-year period', *Developmental Psychology*, 36(2): 241–50. Available online: https://doi.org/10.1037/0012-1649.36.2.241 (accessed 7 July 2023).

Ding, S. and K. Littleton (2005), *Children's Personal and Social Development*, Oxford: Wiley-Blackwell.

Dodd, H.F. and K.J. Lester (2021), 'Adventurous play as a mechanism for reducing risk for childhood anxiety: A conceptual model', *Clinical Child and Family Psychological Review*, 24(1): 164–81. Available online: https://doi.org/10.1007/s10567-020-00338-w (accessed 1 March 2023).

Douch, P. (2020), *The Busker's Guide to Inclusion*, 2nd edn, Eastleigh: Common Threads.

Eager, D. and H. Little (2011), 'Risk deficit disorder', *International Public Works Conference 2011*, Canberra, Australia, 21–25 August 2011.

Egan, S. K. and D. G. Perry (2001), 'Gender identity: A multidimensional analysis with implications for psychoogical adjustment', *Develomental Psychology*, 37(4): 451–63. https://doi.org/10.1037/0012-1649.37.4.451.

Eliot, L. (2010), *Pink Brain Blue Brain*, Oxford: One World Publications.

Elkind, D. (2007), *The Power of Play*, Philadelphia: Da Capo Press.

Ellis, M. (1973), *Why People Play*, Hoboken, NJ: Prentice Hall.

Else, P. (2009), *The Value of Play*, London: Continuum.

Else, P. (2014), *Making Sense of Play: Supporting Children in Their Play*, Maidenhead: Open University Press.

Elwood, B. (2021), 'Longitudinal study suggests Disney princess culture has a positive impact on young children's gender development', *PsyPost*, December 2. Available online: https://www.psypost.org/2021/12/longitudinal-study-suggests-disney-princess-culture-has-a-positive-impact-on-young-childrens-gender-development-62267 (accessed 1 March 2023).

Eveleigh, R. (2022), 'Forest schools are booming in the UK – here's why', *Positive.News*, 7 January. Available online: https://www.positive.news/society/education/forest-schools-are-booming-in-the-uk-heres-why/. (accessed 25 February 2023).

Family and Parenting Institute. (2007), *A Parent's Guide to the Law*, 3rd edn, London: Family and Parenting Institute. Available online: https://www.rbkc.gov.uk/pdf/FPI%20is%20it%20legal%20Feb_08.pdf (accessed 27 February 2023).

Fearns, M. (2020), 'The therapeutic superpowers of play', *Play for Wales*, Spring Issue 55. Available online: https://issuu.com/playwales/docs/play_for_wales_issue_55_spring_2020/s/10538435 (accessed 25 February 2023).

Fisher, J. (2016), *Interacting or Interfering? Improving Interactions in the Early Years*, New York: Open University Press.

Fisher, K. (2008), 'Playwork in the early years: Working in a parallel profession', in F. Brown and C. Taylor (eds), *Foundations of Playwork*, 174–78, Maidenhead: Open University Press.

Fisher, N. (2023), 'Screens, screens, screens', Dr. Naomi Fisher Facebook, 20 January. Available online: https://m.facebook.com/story.php?story_fbid=pfbid0dANui1rrJvwS8FR3zCZdm2uVXiAbJQydzTDCho2kfoXg47RXhwjcXhzGfGbC4NmFland id=100088528062608 (accessed 25 February 2023).

Flannigan, C. and B. Dietze (2018), 'Children, outdoor play, and loose parts', *Journal of Childhood Studies*, 42(4): 53–60 Available online: https://www.researchgate.net/publication/328579135_Children_Outdoor_Play_and_Loose_Parts (accessed 1 March 2023).

Fog Olwig, K. and E. Gulløv (2003), 'Towards an anthropology of children and place', in K. Fog Olwig and E. Gulløv (eds), *Children's Places: Cross-Cultural Perspectives*, 1–19, Abingdon: Routledge.

Fraser, N. (2000), 'Rethinking recognition', *New Left Review*, 3: 107–20.

Frost, J.L. (2010), *A History of Children's Play and Play Environments*, London: Routledge.

Frost, J., S.C. Wortham and R.S. Reifel (2012), *Play and Child Development*, 4th edn, London: Pearson.

Furedi, F. (2006), *Culture of Fear Revisited: Risk-Taking and the Morality of Low Expectation*, 4th edn, London: Continuum.

Garvey, C. (1977), *Play and the Developing Child*, London: Fontana/Open Books and Open Books Publishing.

Geary, D. (2019), 'Sex differences in children's play', *Psychology Today*, 15 October. Available online: https://www.psychologytoday.com/gb/blog/male-female/201910/sex-differences-in-children-s-play (accessed 29 February 2023).

Gentleman, A. (2022), '"An explosion" What is behind rise in girls questioning their gender identity', *The Guardian*, 24 November. Available online: https://

www.theguardian.com/society/2022/nov/24/an-explosion-what-is-behind-the-rise-in-girls-questioning-their-gender-identity (accessed 1 March 2023).

Gibson, E.J. and R.D. Walk (1960), 'The visual cliff', *Scientific American*, 202(4): 64–71. Available online: https://www.jstor.org/stable/24940447 (accessed 5 March 2023).

Gibson, J.J. (1986), *The Ecological Approach to Visual Perception*, Boston, MA: Houghton Mifflin.

Gill, T. (2007), 'No fear growing up in a risk averse society', London: Calouste Gulbenkian Foundation. Available online: https://soscn.org/downloads/library/Play/No_Fear_Growing_Up_in_Risk_Averse_Society.pdf (accessed 27 February 2023).

Gill, T. (2018), 'Playing it safe? A global white paper on risk, liability and children's play in public space'. Available online: https://timrgill.files.wordpress.com/2018/05/bvlf-playingitsafe-04.pdf (accessed 25 February 2023).

Gill, T. and R.M. Miller (2020), 'Play in lockdown: An international study of government and civil society responses to Covid-19 and their impact on children's play and mobility'. Available online: https://ipaworld.org/wp-content/uploads/2020/08/IPA-Covid-report-Final.pdf (accessed 21 November 2022).

Gilmore, H. (2014), '6 lessons kids can teach adults', *Psych Central Newsletter*, Available online: https://psychcentral.com/pro/child-therapist/2014/07/6-lessons-kids-can-teach-adults#1 (accessed 27 February 2023).

Girlguiding. (2015), 'Leading and managing people trainers' toolkit: Managing challenging behaviour in adults'. Available online: https://www.girlguiding.org.uk/globalassets/docs-and-resources/learning-and-development/managing-challenging-behaviour-trainers-toolkit.pdf. (accessed 27 February 2023).

Gittins, D. (1998), *The Child in Question*, London: Macmillan.

Gloucestershire Healthy Living and Learning. (2023), *Play Gloucestershire*. Available online: https://www.ghll.org.uk/partnership-projects/play-gloucestershire/ (accessed 28 February 2023).

Goble, C. and N. Bye-Brooks (2016), *Health & Well-Being for Young People: Building Resilience & Empowerment*, London: Palgrave.

Goleman, D. (1996), *Emotional Intelligence*, London: Bloomsbury.

Golombok, S. (2017), 'Parenting in new family forms', *Current Opinion in Psychology*, 15: 76–80. Available online: https://www.ditchley.com/sites/default/files/2018-09/Golombok%20(2017)%20Current%20Opinion_1.pdf (accessed 1 March 2023).

Goodley, D. and K. Runswick-Cole (2010), 'Emancipating play: Dis/abled children, development and deconstruction', *Disability & Society*, 25(4):

499–512. Available online: https://doi.org/10.1080/09687591003755914 (accessed 25 February 2023).

GOV.UK. (2021), 'Inclusive language: Words to use and avoid when writing about disability', Available online: https://www.gov.uk/government/publications/inclusive-communication/inclusive-language-words-to-use-and-avoid-when-writing-about-disability#:~:text=Use%20'disabled%20people'%20not%20',to%20emphasise%20their%20deaf%20identity (accessed 14 February 2023).

GOV.UK. (2022), 'Holiday activities and food programme 2022'. Available online: https://www.gov.uk/government/publications/holiday-activities-and-food-programme/holiday-activities-and-food-programme-2021 (accessed 21 December 2022).

Gray, P. (2013), *Free to Learn*, New York: Basic Books.

Gray, P. (2014), 'Risky play: Why children love it and need it', *Psychology Today*, April. Available online: https://www.psychologytoday.com/gb/blog/freedom-learn/201404/risky-play-why-children-love-it-and-need-it (accessed 25 February 2023).

Green, J., R. Cross, J. Woodall and K. Tones (2019), *Health Promotion: Planning & Strategies*, 4th edn, London: Sage.

Greenberg, J., J. Schimel and A. Mertens (2002), 'Ageism, denying the face of the future', in T.D. Nelson (ed), *Ageism, Stereotyping and Prejudice Against Older Persons*, 27–48, Cambridge: MIT Press.

Grieshaber, S. and F. McCardle (2010), *The Trouble with Play*, Maidenhead: Open University Press.

Guilbaud, S. (2015), 'Sharing playwork identities: Research across the UK's field of research', *International Journal of Play*, 4(3): 299–315. Available online: https://doi.org/10.1080/21594937.2015.1106052 (accessed 15 March 2023).

Guilbaud, S. (2018), 'The might of play as power and possibility', in F. Brown and B. Hughes (eds), *Aspects of Playwork: Play and Culture Studies*, 107–23, Lanham: Rowman & Littlefield.

Guldberg, H. (2009), *Reclaiming Childhood – Freedom and Play in an Age of Fear*, Oxon: Routledge.

Gülgöz, S., J.J. Glazier, E.A. Enright, D.J. Alonso, L.J. Durwood, A.A. Fast, R. Lowe, J. Chonghui, J. Heer, C.L. Martin and K.R. Olson (2018), 'Similarity in transgender and cisgender children's gender development', *Proceedings of the National Academy of Sciences – PNAS*, 116(49): 24480–5. Available online: https://doi.org/10.1073/pnas.1909367116 (accessed 1 March 2023).

Gurian, M. (2011), *Boys and Girls Learn Differently*, San Francisco: Jossey-Bass.

Halim, M.L., D.N. Ruble, C.S. Tamis-LeMonda, K.M. Zosuls, L.E. Lurye and F.K. Greulich (2014), 'Pink frilly dresses and the avoidance of all things "girly": Children's appearance rigidity and cognitive theories of gender development', *Developmental Psychology*, 50(4): 1091–1101. Available online: https://doi.org/10.1037/a0034906 (accessed 1 March 2023).

Hammack, L., S. Hughes, J. Atwood, E. Cohen, and R. Clark (2022), 'Gender and sexual identity in adolescence: A mixed-methods study of labeling in diverse community settings', *Journal of Adolescent Research*, 37(2): 167–220. Available online: https://journals.sagepub.com/doi/10.1177/07435584211000315 (Accessed 15 July 2023).

Hammond, L. (2003), 'How will the children come home? Emplacement and the creation of the social body in an Ethiopian returnee settlement', in K. Fog Olwig and E. Gulløv, (eds), *Children's Places: Cross-Cultural Perspectives*, 77–96, Abingdon: Routledge.

Hansen, N., C.S. Bialka and S.J. Wong (2022), 'Reading literature about disabled children and adolescents: A window into pre-service teachers' emerging understanding of disability', *Journal of Education for Teaching*, 1–15. Available online: https://doi.org/10.1080/02607476.2022.2126750 (accessed 14 February 2023).

Hart, A., E. Gagnon, S. Eryigit-Madzwamuse, J. Cameron, K. Aranda, A. Rathbone and B. Heaver (2016), 'Uniting resilience research and practice with an inequalities approach', *Sage Open*, 6(4): 1–13. Available online: https://doi.org/10.1177/2158244016682477 (accessed 20 March 2023).

Hartley, T. (2023), 'Harnessing the power of play in coaching', *LinkedIn*, 17 April. Available online: https://www.linkedin.com/pulse/harnessing-power-play-coaching-tom-hartley-1e/ (accessed 23 July 2023).

Harvey, D. (2009), *Cosmopolitanism and Geographies of Freedom*, New York: Columbia University Press.

Harvey, D., C. Loynes, A. Morgan and R. Passy (2021), 'Schools emerging from lockdown: Maximising opportunities for outdoor learning in primary schools', Association for the Study of Primary Education (ASPE) Bulletin, Issue 29, November. Available online: https://www.aspe-uk.eu/wp-content/uploads/2021/12/ASPE-Nov-2021-Bulletin-1.pdf (accessed 25 February 2023).

Hashmi, S., R.E. Vanderwert, A.L. Paine and S.A. Gerson (2022), 'Doll play prompts social thinking and social talking: Representations of internal state language in the brain', *Developmental Science*, 25(2). Available online: https://doi.org/10.1111/desc.13163 (accessed 19 December 2022).

Hattenstone, A. and E. Lawrie (2021), 'Covid: Home-education numbers rise by 75%', *BBC*, 19 July. Available online: https://www.bbc.co.uk/news/education-57255380 (accessed 25 February 2023).

Hatton, A. (2024), 'Researching with children', in D. Fitzgerald and H. Maconochie (eds), *Early Childhood Studies: A Student's Guide*, 2nd edn, 359–72, London: Sage.

Hendricks, B. (2011), *Designing for Play*, 2nd edn, Farnham: Ashgate Publishing.

Henricks, T.S. (2006), *Play Reconsidered*, Urbana and Chicago: University of Illinois Press.

Henricks, T.S. (2009), 'Orderly and disorderly play: A comparison', *American Journal of Play*, 2(1): 12–40. Available online: https://files.eric.ed.gov/fulltext/EJ1069226.pdf (accessed 10 February 2023).

Hodge, N. and K. Runswick-Cole (2013), '"They never pass me the ball": Exposing ableism through the leisure experiences of disabled children, young people and their families', *Children's Geographies*, 11(3): 311–25. Available online: https://doi.org/10.1080/03069885.2012.705817 (accessed 10 February 2023).

Holland, P. (2003), *We Don't Play with Guns Here*, Maidenhead: Open University Press.

Holt, J. (1970), *How Children Learn*, London: Penguin.

Horton, J. and P. Kraftl (2018), 'Three playgrounds: Researching the multiple geographies of children's outdoor play', *Environment and Planning A: Economy and Space*, 50(1): 214–35. Available online: https://doi.org/10.1177/0308518X17735324 (accessed 15 March 2023).

Howard, J. and K. McInnes (2010), 'Thinking through the challenge of a play-based curriculum', in J. Moyles (ed), *Thinking About Play*, 30–44, Maidenhead: Open University Press.

HRC Foundation. (n.d.), 'Sexual orientation and gender identity definition', *Human Rights Campaign Resources*. Available online: https://www.hrc.org/resources/sexual-orientation-and-gender-identity-terminology-and-definitions (accessed 1 March 2023).

Huang, C.J. and I. Brittain (2006), 'Negotiating identities through disability sport', *Sociology of Sport Journal*, 23(4): 352–75. Available online: https://doi.org/10.1123/ssj.23.4.352 (accessed 1 March 2023).

Hubbuck, C. (2020), Reflection, personal communication.

Hughes, B. (1996), *A Playworker's Taxonomy of Play Types*, London: PLAYLINK.

Hughes, B. (2001), *Evolutionary Playwork and Reflective Analytic Practice*. London: Routledge.

Hughes, B. (2002a), *A Playworker's Taxonomy of Play Types*, 2nd edn, London: PLAYLINK.

Hughes, B. (2002b), *The First Claim, Desirable Processes*, Cardiff: Play Wales.

Hughes, B. (2003), 'Play deprivation', in *Play Education Paper: Play Wales*. Available online: https://issuu.com/playwales/docs/play_deprivation (accessed 1 March 2023).

Hughes, B. (2006), *Play Types Speculations and Possibilities*, London: The London Centre for Playwork Education and Training.

Hughes, B. (2012), *Evolutionary Playwork and Reflective Analytic Playwork*, 2nd edn, London: Routledge.

Hughes, B. (2018), 'A quantum of playwork', in F. Brown and B. Hughes (eds), *Aspects of Playwork: Play and Culture Studies*, 193–211, Lanham: Rowman & Littlefield.

Huizinga, J. (1955), *Homo Ludens: A Study of the Play Element in Culture*, Boston: The Beacon Press.

Human Rights Watch. (2021), 'Years don't wait for them – Increased inequalities in children's right to education due to the Covid pandemic', Human Rights Watch, 17 May. Available online: https://www.hrw.org/report/2021/05/17/years-dont-wait-them/increased-inequalities-childrens-right-education-due-covid (accessed 25 February 2023).

Ingold, T. (2011), *Being Alive: Essays on Movement, Knowledge and Description*, London: Routledge.

James, A. and A. James (2012), *Key Concepts in Childhood Studies*, 2nd edn, London: Sage.

Jarvis, P. (2019), 'Perspective 1: The usefulness of play', in A. Brock, P. Jarvis and Y. Olusoga, (eds), *Perspectives on Play: Learning for Life*, 6–16, 3rd edn, London: Routledge.

Jarvis, P., A. Brock and F. Brown (2019), 'Three perspectives on play', in A. Brock, P. Jarvis and Y. Olusoga, (eds), *Perspectives on play: Learning for Life*, 3rd edn, 2–46, London: Routledge.

Jeyasingham, D. (2013), 'The production of spaces in children's social work: Insights from Henri Lefebvre's spatial dialectics', *British Journal of Social Work*, 44(7): 1–16. Available online: https://www.jstor.org/stable/43687769 (accessed 5 May 2022).

Kane, E. (2018), 'Using action research to explore play facilitation in school based, school age childcare settings', in P. King and S. Newstead (eds), *Researching Play from a Playwork Perspective*, 109–22, London: Routledge.

Katch, J. (2001), *Under Deadman's Skin - Discovering the Meaning of Children's Violent Play*, Cambridge: Beacon Press.

Kattan, R.J. and M. Bend (2018), 'Educating for the future: The case of East Asia', *World Bank Blogs*, 12 September. Available online: https://blogs.worldbank.org/education/educating-future-case-east-asia (accessed 25 February 2023).

Keats, J. (1817), 'Letter to George and Tom Keats', 21 December. Available online: https://www.poetryfoundation.org/articles/69384/selections-from-keatss-letters (accessed 25 February 2023).

Kellock, A. and J. Sexton (2018), 'Whose space is it anyway? Learning about space to make space to learn', *Children's Geographies*, 16(2): 115–27. Available online: https://doi.org/10.1080/14733285.2017.1334112 (accessed 5 May 2022).

Kelly-Byrne, D., (1989), *A Child's Play Life: An Ethnographic Study*, New York: Teacher's College Press.

Kids. (2006), *It Doesn't Just Happen: Inclusive Management for Inclusive Play*, London: Kids.

Kilvington, J. and A. Wood (2010), *Reflective Playwork for all Who Work with Children*, London: Continuum.

Kilvington, J. and A. Wood (2016), *Gender, Sex and Children's Play*, London: Bloomsbury Academic.

Kilvington, J. and A. Wood (2018), *Reflective Playwork, for All Who Work with Children*, 2nd edn, London: Bloomsbury Academic.

King, P. and S. Newstead, eds (2018), *Researching Play from a Playwork Perspective*, London: Routledge.

King, P. and S. Newstead (2022), 'Childcare worker's understanding of the play cycle theory: Can a focus on "process not product" contribute to quality childcare experiences?', *Child Care in Practice: Northern Ireland Journal of Multi-Disciplinary Child Care Practice*, 28(2): 164–77. Available online: https://doi.org/10.1080/13575279.2019.1680532 (accessed 10 March 2023).

Kingston-Hughes, B. (2022), *A Very Unusual Journey into Play*, London: Corwin.

Knight, S. (2016), *Forest School in Practice for All Ages*, London: Sage.

Kohlberg, L. (1966), 'Cognitive stages and preschool education', *Human Development*, 9: 5–17. Available online: https://www.jstor.org/stable/26761699 (accessed 1 March 2023).

Korczak, J. ([1925] 1992), *When I Am Little Again and the Child's Right to Respect*, trans. E.P. Kulaweic, Lanham: University Press of America.

Kruk, E. (2015), 'What exactly is "the best interest of the child"? The essential needs of children after parental divorce', *Psychology Today*, 22 February. Available online: https://www.psychologytoday.com/gb/blog/co-parenting-after-divorce/201502/what-exactly-is-the-best-interest-the-child (accessed 27 February 2023).

Lawler, S. (2014), *Identity: Sociological Perspectives*, 2nd edn, Cambridge: Polity Press.

Lefebvre, H. (1991), *The Production of Space*, Oxford: Blackwell

Leigh, J. (2017), 'Experiencing emotion: Children's perceptions, reflections and self-regulation', *Body, Movement and Dance in Psychotherapy*, 12(2): 128–44. Available online: https://doi.org/10.1080/17432979.2017.1303544 (accessed 1 March 2023).

Lester, S. (2008), 'Play and the play stage', in F. Brown and C. Taylor (eds), *Foundations of Playwork*, 55–58, Maidenhead: Open University Press.

Lester, S. (2018), 'Playwork and the co-creation of play spaces: The rhythms and refrains of a play environment', in F. Brown and B. Hughes (eds), *Aspects of Playwork: Play and Culture Studies*, Vol. 14, 79–92, Lanham: Rowman & Littlefield.

Lester, S. (2020), *Everyday Playfulness: A New Approach to Children's Play and Adult Responses to It*, London: Jessica Kingsley Publishers.

Lester, S. and W. Russell (2008), *Play for a Change: Play, Policy and Practice: A Review of Contemporary Perspectives*, London: National Children's Bureau.

Lester, S. and W. Russell (2013), 'Utopian visions of childhood and play in English social policy', in A. Parker and D. Vinson (eds), *Youth, Sport, Physical Activity and Play*, 40–52, New York: Routledge.

Lester, S. and W. Russell (2014), 'Turning the world upside down: Playing as the deliberate creation of uncertainty', *Children*, 1(2): 241–60. Available online: https://doi.org/10.3390%2Fchildren1020241 (accessed 10 March 2023).

Lester, S., W. Russell, W. and H. Smith, eds (2017), *Practice Based Research in Children's Play*, London: Policy Press.

Liu, C., L. Solis, H. Jensen, E.J. Hopkins, D. Neale, J.M. Zosh, K. Hirsh-Pasek and D. Whitebread (2017), *Neuroscience and Learning Through Play: A Review of the Evidence (Research Summary)*, The LEGO Foundation. Available online: https://doi.org/10.13140/RG.2.2.11789.84963 (accessed 10 December 2022).

Loewen, J. (1996), 'Intergenerational learning: What if schools were places where adults and children learned together?' US Department of Education. Available online: https://files.eric.ed.gov/fulltext/ED404014.pdf (accessed 29 March 2023).

Lorimer, H. (2005), 'Cultural Geography: The busyness of being "more-than-representational"', *Progress in Human Geography*, 29(1): 83–94. Available online: https://doi.org/10.1191/0309132505ph531pr (accessed 5 May 2022).

Ludicology. (2019), 'Play as an outcome', *Ludicology*, Available online: https://ludicology.com/store-room/play-as-an-outcome/ (accessed 1 June 2022).

Maccoby, E.E. (2003), *The Two Sexes – Growing Up Apart – Coming Together*, Cambridge: The Belknap Press.

Manwaring, B. and C. Taylor (2007), *The Benefits of Play and Playwork: Recent Evidence-based Research (2001–2006) Demonstrating the Impact and Benefits of Play and Playwork*, London: The Community and Youth Workers' Union and SkillsActive.

Marsh, J., L. Plowman, D. Yamada-Rice, J. Bishop and F. Scott (2016), 'Digital play: A new classification', *Early Years*, 36(3): 242–53. Available online: https://doi.org/10.1080/09575146.2016.1167675 (accessed 27 February 2023).

Martin, B. (2011), *Children at Play – Learning Gender in the Early Years*, London: Institute of Education Press.

Martin, C. (2017a), 'Play and digital technology', *Play Wales*. Available online: https://issuu.com/playwales/docs/play_and_digital_technology (accessed 21 August 2023).

Martin, C. (2017b), 'Children, mobile phones and outdoor play', in W. Russell, H. Smith and S. Lester (eds), *Practice-Based Research in Children's Play*, 167–83, Bristol: Policy Press.

Martin, C.L. and D.N. Ruble (2010), 'Patterns of gender development', *Annual Review of Psychology*, 61: 353–81. Available online: https://www.ncbi.nlm.nih.gov/pmc/articles/PMC3747736/ (accessed 1 March 2023).

Martin, C.L. and D. Ruble (2004), 'Children's search for gender cues: Cognitive perspectives on gender development', *Current Directions in Psychological Science*, 13(2): 67–70. Available online: https://doi.org/10.1111/j.0963-7214.2004.00276.x (accessed 1 March 2023).

Martin, C., R. Fabes and L. Hanish (2014), 'Gendered peer relationships in educational contexts', *Advances in Child Development and Behavior*, 47: 151–87. Available online: https://doi.org/10.1016/bs.acdb.2014.04.002 (accessed 28 February 2023).

Masten, A.S. (2007), 'Resilience in developing systems: Progress and promise as the fourth wave rises', *Development and Psychopathology*, 19(3): 921–30. Available online: https://doi.org/10.1017/S0954579407000442 (accessed 25 February 2023).

Masten, A.S. (2011), 'Resilience in children threatened by extreme adversity: Frameworks for research, practice, and translational synergy', *Development and Psychopathology*, 23(2): 493–506. Available online: https://doi.org/10.1017/S0954579411000198 (accessed 25 February 2023).

Mayall, B. (2008), 'Conversations with children: Working with generational issues', in P.M. Christensen and A. James (eds), *Research with Children: Perspectives and Practices*, 2nd edn, 109–24, London: Routledge.

Mayeza, E.S. (2015), 'Playing gender in childhood: How boys and girls construct and experience schooling and play in a township primary school near Durban', PhD diss., Stellenbosch University, South Africa. Available online: https://scholar.sun.ac.za/browse?type=author&value=Mayeza%2C+Emmanuel+Simo (accessed 28 February 2023).

Meares, C. (2021), Reflection, shoot the Prime Minister, personal communication.

Meares, C. and P. Keeling (2016), *A Playwork Approach to Resilience: Strengthening Communities, Summary Report for MAPA*, Birmingham: MAPA.

Miller, S. (1974), 'The playful, the crazy and the nature of pretence', *Rice University Studies*, 60(3): 31–51.

Moss, P. (2010), *UNESCO Policy Brief on Early Childhood*, 47/2010, Thomas Coran Research Unit.

Moyles, J.R. (1989), *Just Playing? The Role and Status of Play in Early Childhood Education*, Milton Keynes: Open University Press.

Moyles, J.R., ed. (2010), *Thinking About Play*, Maidenhead: Open University Press.

Muller-Mahn, D., J. Everts and C. Stephan (2018), 'Riskscapes revisited – Exploring the relationship between risk, space and practice', *Erdkunde*, 72(3): 197–213. Available online: https://doi.org/10.3112/erdkunde.2018.02.09 (accessed 25 February 2023).

National Fostering Group (2018), '9 Behavioural management strategies for parents and foster carers'. Available online https://www.nfa.co.uk/story/blog-news/9-behavioural-management-strategies-you-can-use-at-home/ (accessed 27 February 2023).

Neill, A.S. (1962), Summerhill, Harmondsworth: Penguin.

Newson, J. and E. Newson (1979), *Toys and Playthings*, London: Allen & Unwin.

Newstead, S. (2004), *The Buskers Guide to Playwork*, Eastleigh: Common Threads.

Newstead, S. (2018), 'Playwork research as the art of mirroring', in P. King and S. Newstead (eds), *Researching Play from a Playwork Perspective*, 25–38, London: Routledge.

Nijhof, S.L., C.H. Vinkers, S.M. van Geelen, S.N. Duijff, E.J.M. Achterberg, J. van der Net, R.C. Veltkamp, M.A. Grootenhuis, E.M. van de Putte, M.H.J. Hillegers, A.W. van der Brug, C.J. Wierenga, M.J.N.L. Benders, R.C.M.E. Engels, C.K. van der Ent, L.J.M.J. Vanderschuren and H.M.B. Lesscher (2018), 'Healthy play, better coping: The importance of play for the development of children in health and disease', *Neuroscience and Biobehavioral Reviews*, 95: 421–9. Available online: https://doi.org/10.1016/j.neubiorev.2018.09.024 (accessed 24 February 2023).

Nin, A. (1961), *Seduction of the Minotaur*, Chicago: The Swallow Press.

Olusoga, Y. (2019), '"We don't play like that here" Social, cultural and gender perspectives on play,' in A. Brock, P. Jarvis, and Y. Olusoga (eds), *Perspectives on Play. Learning for Life*, 3rd edn, 47–80, London: Routledge.

Opie, P. and I. Opie (1969), *Children's Games in Street and Playground*, Oxford: Oxford University Press.

Orbach, S. (1994), *What's Really Going on Here?* London: Virago.

Outdoor Classroom Day. (n.d.), 'Outdoor classroom day'. Available online: https://outdoorclassroomday.org.uk/ (accessed 25 February 2023).

Panjwani, S., S. Anderson-Badbade, M. Oo, I. Velez and J. Beckham (2022), 'Play promotion for pediatric patients: A feasibility and pilot study of embedding "prescription for play" in well-child visits, phase 1 evaluation report', Middleton, CT: Weitzman Institute, Community Health Center, Inc. Available online: https://www.weitzmaninstitute.org/wp-content/uploads/2022/04/P4P-Phase-1-Final-Report.pdf (accessed 3 March 2023).

Panksepp, J. (1998), *Affective Neuroscience the Foundations of Human and Animal Emotions*, New York: Oxford University Press.

Panksepp, J. (2000). 'The riddle of laughter: Neural and psychoevolutionary underpinnings of joy', *Current Directions in Psychological Science*, 9(6): 183–6. Available online: https://doi.org/10.1111/1467-8721.00090 (accessed 3 March 2023).

Pardhan, S., J. Parkin, M. Trott and R. Driscoll (2022), 'Risks of digital screen time and recommendations for mitigating adverse outcomes in children and adolescents', *The Journal of School Health*, 92(8): 765–73. Available online: https://doi.org/10.1111/josh.13170 (accessed 1 January 2023).

Pellegrini, A.D. (2005), *Recess: Its Role in Education and Development*, New York: Psychology Press.

Pellegrini, A.D. (2009), *The Role of Play in Human Development*, Oxford: Oxford University Press.

Pellis, S.M. and V. Pellis (2009), *The Playful Brain: Venturing to the Limits of Neuroscience*, London: Oneworld Publications.

Pellis, S.M., E. Hastings, T. Shimizu, H. Kamitakahara, J. Komorowska, M.L Forgie and B. Kolb (2006), 'The effects of orbital frontal cortex damage on the modulation of defensive responses by rats in playful and nonplayful social contexts', *Behavioral Neuroscience*, 120(1): 72–84. Available online: https://doi.org/10.1037/0735-7044.120.1.72 (accessed 20 February 2023).

Penn State. (2022), 'Transgender parents bring child-centred perspective to parenthood, research finds: Transgender parents may let children explore gender on their own before labeling child's identity', *ScienceDaily*, 2 September. Available online: www.sciencedaily.com/releases/2022/09/220902111337.htm (accessed 1 March 2023).

Piaget, J. (1962), *Play, Dreams, and Imitation in Childhood*, New York: Norton.

Play Gloucestershire. (2021), *Play Nurture Plus Handbook*. Available online: https://playgloucestershire.org.uk/wp-content/uploads/2022/05/PG-Play-Nurture-Plus-Handbook-2021-22.pdf (accessed 11 March 2023).

Play Gloucestershire. (2023), *Play Nurture*. Available online: https://playgloucestershire.org.uk/play-nurture-gloucestershire/ (accessed 11 March 2023).

Play Wales. (2008), 'Participation and playwork', *Play for Wales*, Spring (24). Available online: https://www.yumpu.com/en/document/view/25388863/participation-and-playwork-roger-hartpdf-play-wales (accessed 20 February 2023).

Play Wales. (2020a), *Thinking About Loose Parts in School*. Available online: https://www.playwales.org.uk/login/uploaded/documents/INFORMATION%20SHEETS/Thinking%20about%20loose%20parts%20in%20school%202020.pdf.(accessed 25 February 2023).

Play Wales. (2020b), *A Play Friendly School – Guidance for a Whole School Approach*. Available online: https://www.playwales.org.uk/login/uploaded/

documents/Schools/Schools%20guidance/A%20play%20friendly%20school%202020.pdf (accessed 25 February 2023).

Play Wales. (2023), 'The inclusion debate', Available online: https://www.playwales.org.uk/eng/inclusiondebate (accessed 1 March 2023).

Playwork Principles Scrutiny Group. (2005), *Playwork Principles*, Cardiff: Play Wales.

Plowden, B. (1967), *Children and Their Primary Schools: A Report of the Central Advisory Council of Education England*, London: HMSO.

Powell, S. (2009), 'The value of play: Constructions of play in government policy in England', *Children and Society*, 23: 29–42. Available online: https://doi.org/10.1111/j.1099-0860.2008.00137.x (accessed 15 January 2023).

Priess, H. and J. Shibley Hyde (2011), 'Binary and gradient views of gender segregation', *Encyclopedia of Adolescence*. Available online: https://www.sciencedirect.com/topics/psychology/gender-segregation (accessed 1 March 2023).

Pringle, M.K. (1986), *The Needs of Children*, London: Hutchinson

Putnam, R.D. (2000), *Bowling Alone: The Collapse and Revival of American Community*, New York: Simon & Schuster.

Reimers, A., S. Schoeppe, Y. Demetriou and G. Knapp (2018), 'Physical activity and outdoor play of children in public playgrounds—do gender and social environment matter?' *International Journal of Environmental Research and Public Health*, 15(7): 1–14. Available online: https://www.genderopen.de/bitstream/handle/25595/533/ReimersSchoeppeDemetriouKnapp_2018_PublicPlaygrounds.pdf?sequence=3 (accessed 1 March 2023).

Rennie, S. (2003), 'Making play work: The fundamental role of play in the development of social relationship skills', in F. Brown (ed), *Playwork theory and Practice*, 18–31, Buckingham: Open University Press.

Rich-Harris, J. (1999), *The Nurture Assumption*, New York: Touchstone.

Rix, S. (2016), Reflection, personal communication.

Robinson, M. (2010). *Understanding Behaviour and Development in Early Childhood: A Guide to Theory and Practice*, London: Routledge.

Rogoff, B. (1990), *Apprenticeship in Thinking*, Oxford: Oxford University Press.

Roisman, G.L., E. Padrón, L.A. Sroufe and B. Egeland (2002), 'Earned-secure attachment status in retrospect and prospect', *Child Development*, 73(4): 1204–19. Available online: https://doi.org/10.1111/1467-8624.00467 (accessed 25 February 2023).

Russell, H. (2021), 'Lego to remove gender bias from its toys after findings of child survey', *The Guardian*, 11 October. Available online: https://www.theguardian.com/lifeandstyle/2021/oct/11/lego-to-remove-gender-bias-after-survey-shows-impact-on-children-stereotypes (accessed 1 March 2023).

Russell, W. (2005), 'The unnatural art of playwork', in G. Sturrock, P. Else and W. Russell (eds), *Therapeutic Playwork Reader 2 (2000–5)*, 96–105, Sheffield: Ludemos.

Russell, W. (2006), *Reframing Playwork Reframing Challenging Behaviour*, Nottingham: Nottingham City Council.

Russell, W. (2008), 'Modelling playwork: Brawgs continuum, dialogue and collaborative reflection', in F. Brown and C. Taylor (eds), *Foundations of Playwork*, 84–8, Maidenhead: Open University Press.

Russell, W. (2010), 'Playwork', in T. Bruce (ed), *Early Childhood: A Guide for Students*, 312–24, London: Sage.

Russell, W. (2012), 'I get such a feeling out of…those moments: Playwork, passion, politics and space', *International Journal of Play*, 1(1): 51–63. Available online: https://doi.org/10.1080/21594937.2012.656921 (accessed 5 May 2022).

Russell, W. (2018), 'Nonsense, caring and everyday hope: Rethinking the value of playwork', in F. Brown and B. Hughes (eds), *Aspects of Playwork: Play & Culture Studies*, Vol. 14, 13–28, Lanham: Rowman & Littlefield.

Russell, W., M. Barclay and B. Tawil (2023), 'Playing and being well: A review of recent research into children's play, social policy and practice', with a focus on Wales. Briefing, Play Wales. Available online: https://play.wales/wp-content/uploads/2023/06/Playing-and-being-well-briefing.pdf (accessed 24 July 2023).

Rutter, M. (2006), 'The promotion of resilience in the face of adversity', in A. Clarke-Stewart and J. Dunn (eds), *Families Count: Effects on Child and Adolescent Development*, 26–52, Cambridge: Cambridge University Press.

Sandseter, E.B. (2007), 'Categorising risky play – How can we identify risk-taking in children's play?', *European Early Childhood Education Research Journal*, 15(2): 237–52. Available online: https://doi.org/10.1080/13502930701321733 (accessed 25 February 2023).

Sandseter, E.B. (2022), 'A GoPro look on how children aged 17–25 months assess and manage risk during free exploration in a varied natural environment', *Education Sciences*, 12(5): 361. Available online: https://doi.org/10.3390/educsci12050361 (accessed 25 February 2023).

Sandseter, E.B.H. and L.E.O. Kennair (2011), 'Children's risky play from an evolutionary perspective', *Evolutionary Psychology*, 9(2): 257–84. Available online: https://doi.org/10.1177/147470491100900212 (accessed 25 February 2023).

Savage, K. (2015), 'Children, young people, inclusion and social policy', in K. Brodie and K. Savage (eds), *Inclusion and Early Years Practice*, 1–17, London: Routledge.

Sax, L. (2005), *Why Gender Matters*, New York: Broadway Books.

Selhub, E. and A. Logan (2014), *Your Brain on Nature*, Toronto: John Wiley & Sons.

Shooter, M. (2020), 'Guest editorial', *Play and Being Well,* 55, Spring edition Available online: /https://issuu.com/playwales/docs/play_for_wales_issue_55_spring_2020?fr=sZGZkYzEzOTYxMTA (accessed 25 February 2023).

Sigman, A. (2015), *Play - It's in Their DNA. A Report by Dr Aric Sigman Commissioned for the Make Time 2 Play Campaign*, 25 August. Available online: https://www.maketime2play.co.uk/wp-content/uploads/2015/08/PLAY-Its-in-their-DNA.pdf (accessed 20 January 2023).

Singer, D.G. and J.L. Singer (2005), *Imagination and Play in the Electronic Age*, Cambridge, MA: Harvard University Press.

Singer, D., R. Golinkoff and K. Hirsh-Pasek (2006), *Play = Learning: How Play Motivates and Enhances Children's Cognitive and Social-Emotional Growth*, Oxford: Oxford University Press.

Smith, F. and J. Barker (2000), 'Contested spaces: Children's experiences of out of school care in England and Wales', *Childhood*, 7(3): 315–33. Available online: https://doi.org/10.1177/0907568200007003005 (accessed 1 June 2022).

Smith, P. (2010), *Children and Play*, Chichester: Wiley-Blackwell.

Smith, P.K. and A.D. Pellegrini (2005), *The Nature of Play: Great Apes and Humans*, New York: Guildford Press.

Southam-Gerow, M. (2013), *Emotion Regulation in Children and Adolescents*, London: Guildford Press.

Spencer, C. and M. Blades (2006), 'An introduction', in C. Spencer and M. Blades (eds), *Children and Their Environments*, 1–12, Cambridge: Cambridge University Press.

Spencer, H. (1904), *An Autobiography*, Vol. 1, New York: D. Appleton.

Spinka M., R.C. Newberry and M. Bekoff (2001), 'Mammalian play: Training for the unexpected', *Quarterly Review Biology*, 76(2): 141–68. Available online: https://doi.org/10.1086/393866 (accessed 1 June 2022).

Sroufe, L.A. (1997), *Emotional Development*, Cambridge: Cambridge University Press.

Sturrock, G. (2002), 'The idea of unplayed out material', in G. Sturrock, P. Else and W. Russell (eds), *Therapeutic Playwork Reader 2 (2000–5)*, Sheffield: Ludemos.

Sturrock, G. (2007), 'Towards the tenets of playwork practice', *IpDip*, 1(17): i–iv, Eastbourne Playwork Development and Training Community Interest Company.

Sturrock, G. and P. Else (1998), *The Playground as a Therapeutic Space: Playwork as Healing*, Sheffield: Ludemos Associates.

Suomi, S.J. and H.F. Harlow (1971), 'Monkeys without play', in J.S. Bruner, A. Jolly and K. Sylva (eds), *Play: Its Role in Development and Evolution*, 787–95, New York: Basic Books.

Sutton-Smith, B. (1997), *The Ambiguity of Play*, Boston: Harvard University Press.

Sutton-Smith, B. (2003), *The Ambiguity of Play*, 2nd edn, Cambridge: Harvard University Press.

Sutton-Smith, B. (2009), *The Ambiguity of Play*, 2nd edn, Cambridge: Harvard University Press. Available online: https://www.perlego.com/book/1133144/the-ambiguity-of-play-pdf (accessed 27 March 2023).

Sutton-Smith, B. (2017), *Play for Life: Play Theory and Play as Emotional Survival*, New York: The Strong.

Tambalis, K.D., D.B. Panagiotakos, G. Psarra and L.S. Sidossis (2020), 'Screen time and its effect on dietary habits and lifestyle among school children', *Central European Journal of Public Health*, 28(4): 260–6. Available online: https://doi.org/10.21101/cejph.a6097 (accessed 2 January 2023).

Teachwire. (2023), 'Behaviour management strategies – 15 tips and ideas for early years'. Available online: https://www.teachwire.net/news/behaviour-management-for-early-years/ (accessed 27 February 2023).

Tenenbaum, H.R. and C. Leaper (2002), 'Are parents' gender schemas related to their children's gender-related cognitions? A meta-analysis', *Developmental Psychology*, 38(4): 615–30. Available online: https://pubmed.ncbi.nlm.nih.gov/12090490/ (accessed 1 March 2023).

The Children's Society. (2020), *Good Childhood Report 2020*. Available online: https://www.childrenssociety.org.uk/sites/default/files/2020-11/Good-Childhood-Report-2020.pdf (accessed 2 February 2023).

Thorne, B. (1993), *Gender Play – Girls and Boys in School*, Berkshire: Open University Press.

Thorne, B. and Z. Luria (1986), 'Sexuality and gender in children's daily worlds', *Social Problems*, 33(3): 176–90. Available online: https://doi.org/10.1525/sp.1986.33.3.03a00020 (accessed 1 March 2023).

Tuan, Y-F. (1974), *Topophilia: A Study of Environmental Perception, Attitudes and Values*, Englewood Cliffs: Prentice-Hall.

Twenge, J.M. (2000), 'The age of anxiety? The birth cohort change in anxiety and neuroticism', *Journal of Personality and Social Psychology*, 79(6): 1007–1021. Available online: https://doi.org/10.1037/0022-3514.79.6.1007 (accessed 25 February 2023).

Twiselton, S., J. Blake, B. Francis, R. Gill, M. Harmer, E. Hollis, R. Moore and J.N. Rogers (2019), *Initial Teacher Training (ITT): Core Framework*, London: Department for Education. Available online: https://assets.publishing.service.gov.uk/government/uploads/system/uploads/attachment_data/file/974307/ITT_core_content_framework_.pdf. (accessed 25 February 2023).

Underdown, A. (2007), *Young Children's Health and Well-Being*. Maidenhead: Open University Press.

Ungar, M. (2008), 'Resilience across cultures', *British Journal of Social Work*, 38(2): 218–35. Available online: https://doi.org/10.1093/bjsw/bcl343. (accessed 25 February 2023).

Ungar, M. (2012), *The Social Ecology of Resilience*, New York: Springer.

Ungar, M. (2013), 'Resilience, trauma, context, and culture', *Trauma, Violence, & Abuse*, 14(3): 255–66. Available online: https://doi.org/10.1177/1524838013487805 (accessed 25 February 2023).

Ungar, M. (2015), 'Resilience and culture: The diversity of protective processes and positive adaptation', in L.C. Theron, L. Liebenberg and M. Ungar (eds), *Youth Resilience and Culture*, 37–48, Dordrecht: Springer.

UNICEF. (1989), 'United nations convention on the rights of the child'. Available online: https://www.unicef.org.uk/what-we-do/un-convention-child-rights/ (accessed 8 February 2023).

UNICEF. (1990), 'The united nations convention on the rights of the child', UNICEF. Available online: https://www.unicef.org.uk/what-we-do/un-convention-child-rights/ (accessed 28 February 2023).

Uprichard, E. (2008), 'Children as "beings and becomings": Children, childhood and temporality', *Children and Society*, 22(4): 303–13. Available online: https://doi.org/10.1111/j.1099-0860.2007.00110.x (accessed 14 February 2023).

US National Centre on Parent, Family and Community Engagement. (n.d.), 'Healthy gender development and young children a guide for early childhood programs and professionals', US, Department of Health and Human Services, Administration for Children and Families, Office of Head Start and Office of Child Care. Available online: https://depts.washington.edu/dbpeds/healthy-gender-development.pdf (accessed 1 March 2023).

Vaughn, A. (2013), 'Four out of five UK children 'not connected to nature', *The Guardian*, 16 October. Available online: https://www.theguardian.com/environment/2013/oct/16/uk-children-not-connected-nature-rspb (accessed 1 March 2023).

Vygotsky, L.S. (1978), *Mind in Society: The Development of Higher Psychological Processes*, Cambridge: Harvard University Press.

Waldner-Haugrud, L. and B. Macgruder (1996), 'Homosexual identity expression among lesbian and gay adolescents: An analysis of perceived structural associations', *Youth & Society*, 27(3): 313–333. Available online: https://www.researchgate.net/publication/249684302_Homosexual_Identity_Expression_among_Lesbian_and_Gay_Adolescents_An_Analysis_of_Perceived_Structural_Associations (accessed 28 February 2023).

Ward, C. (1979), *The Child in the City*, Harmondsworth: Penguin.

Webb, N.B. (2015), *Play Therapy with Children and Adolescents in Crisis*, 4th edn, London: The Guildford Press.

Webb, S. and F. Brown (2003), 'Playwork in adversity: Working with abandoned children in Romania', in F. Brown (ed), *Playwork: Theory and Practice*, 157–75, Buckingham: Open University Press.

WHO. (1986), 'Ottawa charter for health promotion', Geneva: WHO. Available online: https://www.euro.who.int/__data/assets/pdf_file/0004/129532/Ottawa_Charter.pdf (accessed 1 January 2023).

Williams-Brown, Z. and M. Jopling (2020), 'Measuring a plant doesn't help it to grow: Teachers' perspectives on the standards agenda in England', *Education 3-13*, 49(2): 227–40. Available online: https://doi.org/10.1080/03004279.2020.1717573 (accessed 25 February 2023).

Wilson, P. (2020), Reflection, personal communication.

Wingrave, M. (2014), 'An old issue in a new era: "Early years practitioners perceptions of gender"', Doctoral diss., University of Glasgow, Glasgow.

Wood, E. and J. Attwood (1996), *Play, Learning and the Early Childhood Curriculum*, London: Paul Chapman Publishing.

Wragg, M. (2011), 'The child's right to play: Rhetoric or reality?', in P. Jones and G. Walker (eds), *Children's Rights in Practice*, 71–81, London: Sage.

Wragg, M. (2018), 'The neoliberalism of childhood and the future of playwork', in F. Brown and B. Hughes (eds), *Aspects of Playwork: Play & Culture Studies*, Vol. 14, 29–42, Lanham: Rowman & Littlefield.

Yogman, M., A. Garner, J. Hutchinson, K. Hirsh-Pasek, R. Michnick Golinkoff, Committee on Psychosocial Aspects of Child and Family Health and Council on Communications and Media. (2018), 'The power of play: A pediatric role in enhancing development in young children', *Pediatrics*, 142(3): 1–16. Available online: https://doi.org/10.1542/peds.2018-2058 (accessed 25 February 2023).

Zhao, Z. (2017), 'The West and Asian education', *New Internationalist*, 1 September. Available online: https://newint.org/features/2017/09/01/asian-education (accessed 25 February 2023).

Zinn, J. (2016), 'The meaning of risk taking – key concepts and dimensions', *Journal of Risk Research*, 22(1): 1–15. Available online: https://www.tandfonline.com/doi/full/10.1080/13669877.2017.1351465 (accessed 1 June 2022).

Index

Adulteration   18, 19
affective atmosphere   48, 60, 81
affordances   13, 83, 149
amygdala   104, 105
Andrews, M.   40, 43, 44
Ardelean, A.   47, 50
assemblage   16, 31, 85
attainment   57, 122
Aumann, K.   97

Ball, D.   90
Barclay, M.   89, 96, 98, 120
barriers   58, 63, 67
becoming child   1, 59, 60, 143, 144
behaviour management   23
being child   1, 59, 60, 129, 143, 144
belonging   15, 58, 60, 61, 67, 72, 81, 109
brain development   125, 131
Briggs, M.   51
Brock, A.   43
Brown, F.   2, 10, 11, 17, 40, 46, 50, 75, 78, 108, 110, 111, 113, 125, 129, 153

Cattanach, A.   113, 117
chaotic response   76
characteristics of playful experiences   125, 131
children, disabled   56–8, 63, 65, 67
co-create   4, 9, 60, 79, 83, 85, 128
co-creation   74, 85
cognitive dissonance   51, 52
communication play   23, 127
contemporary play   32, 96
Conway, M.   131

Cullen, F.   5, 6, 52
culture   56, 57

deaf people   68
deferred benefits   123
Deleuze, G.   85
democratic schools   51, 52
den-building   77, 78
didactic response   76
Dietz, B.   150
Dodd, H.   90
dynamics power
   adult   2, 6, 15, 59
   adult/child   24, 60, 64, 75, 78, 79, 113
   of play   9, 17, 18, 24, 32, 35, 42, 52, 53, 59, 60, 64, 117, 153

education
   current trends in   39
   exam-oriented   41
   formal   10, 28, 38, 114
   home   39
Else, P.   10, 59, 66, 79, 133, 134
emotional
   development   11, 103, 104, 109, 110, 123
   regulation   97, 108, 117, 126
   risks   96
emotions
   empathy   95, 104
   primary   104, 105
   secondary   105
environments
   outdoor   149, 150

play 2, 7, 10, 12, 16, 19, 43, 46, 48, 58
playful 32, 46, 53, 83, 85
exclusion 21, 56, 115

femininity 135, 147
Fisher, J. 43, 53, 96, 114
Flannigan, C. 150
Forest School 50
freedom 5, 13, 26, 51, 68, 75, 97, 109, 110, 112, 113, 117, 131, 150
functional near-infrared spectroscopy 125
Furedi, F. 88

gender and toys 141, 144–9, 151
gender identity 135–7, 141, 143, 144, 148, 149
Gentleman, A. 141
Gibson, J. 83, 95
Gill, T. 35, 88, 90, 99, 122
Good Childhood Report 139
good risks 88
Goodley, D. 58, 59
Gray, P 40, 42
Grieshaber, S. 8, 10, 23, 43, 115
Guattari, F. 85
Gulgoz, S, et al. 148

Halim, M, et al. 138
Hansen, A. 51
Hart, A, et al. 96, 97
hazard 87
health and safety 30, 87, 88, 91, 93, 132
Henricks, T. 6, 9, 10, 21
hierarchy 56, 59–61, 113, 153
Hughes, B. 4, 10, 13, 31, 32, 34, 36, 79, 89, 112, 133

identity-first language 67
immediate benefits 123, 129
inclusion 55–7, 59, 60, 63–5, 67

inclusive practice 56, 62, 68, 150
independence 25, 97, 98, 110
instrumental aspects of play 4
instrumental value of play 47, 78, 124, 129
intervention
  approaches 25
  methods 19, 23
  playwork intervention 25, 30
  unnecessary 35, 62
intra-action 85
intrinsic value of play 3, 14, 48, 79

Jarvis, P. 6, 40, 43, 78
Johnston, C. 5, 6, 52
joy 5, 26, 29, 101, 125, 130, 131

Kellock, A. 71
Kelly-Byrne, D. 26
Kilvington, J. 8, 10, 13, 19, 25, 27, 30, 36, 42, 123, 133–5, 144, 147, 150
Knight, S. 46, 50

language
  community languages 66–8
  gendered language 148, 150
  language of play 108, 114
  person first language 67
Lawler, S. 27
learning
  adult directed 40, 42, 131
  outdoor 39, 45, 46, 51
Lester, R. 90
Lester, S. 2–5, 9, 10, 13, 22, 25, 31, 64, 75, 76, 80, 85, 86, 88, 90, 97, 106, 108, 120, 125, 131, 134
lockdowns 121, 122
Long, A. 2, 11, 17, 75, 153
loose parts 13, 31, 32, 45, 46, 49, 79, 83, 110, 146, 149, 150
Ludicology 11
ludocentric response 76

McCardle, F. 8, 10, 23, 43, 115
Makaton 64, 65
Marsh, J, et al. 31, 32, 96
Martin, B. 96, 137, 140, 147
masculinity 135, 139, 147
matterings 61
medical model of disability 63
Meriden Adventure Playground 62, 88, 97, 98, 124
Moyles, J. 40, 42

negative capability 11, 17, 52, 53
Neill, A 51
NHS Birmingham and Solihull 124
NHS Gloucestershire 123
non-disabled 56–8
normative 63, 104

Olusoga, Y. 43
Opie, I. 70
Opie, P. 70
outcomes of playing 1, 3, 11, 12, 17, 19, 59

Panksepp, J 105, 125
Pellegrini, A 5, 25, 41, 131
Pellis, S. 125
Pellis, V. 125
permission for play 32, 44, 48, 49, 98
personal pronouns 150
physical exercise 122
Pitsmoor Adventure Playground 67, 83, 84, 130
planning for play 5, 53
play
   behaviour 2, 4, 9, 12, 21, 31, 35, 137–8
   cues 21, 65, 66, 79
   deep 89, 90, 99, 102, 105, 108
   deprivation 42, 95, 112
   digital 31, 32, 95, 96, 121
   disorderly 6, 21, 22
   exploratory 31, 79, 117

free 48, 50, 98, 108, 112, 122, 130, 131
   knowledge 147
   mastery 50, 79, 105, 108, 113
   nurture 38, 112
   object 31, 79
   orderly 6, 21, 22
   orientation 136, 137
   playful responses 36
   playwork approach 62, 79
   sexual development 133, 134, 139
   support for play 5, 9, 23, 44, 53, 59, 76, 112, 113, 124, 132, 133
play as a process 129
Play Gloucestershire 124
play out 13, 90, 113, 145
play-based education 43
playful atmosphere 2, 10, 35, 83, 85
playful attitude 44, 45, 53
playful responses 19, 25, 33, 34, 36
playfulness 9, 32, 44, 53, 72, 76
playing out 103, 113, 150
playspacetimes 4, 85
playwork
   intervention 2, 10, 19, 23–5, 30, 34, 35, 62, 153
   Principle 1 57
   Principle 2 58, 132
   Principle 5 72, 74
posthumanism 61, 83

reflection 2, 8, 15, 16, 18, 19, 34, 50, 58, 62–4, 69–74, 80, 94, 105, 143, 149, 153
relational capability approach 120
resilience 43, 52, 96–8, 106, 108–12, 117, 122, 123, 132
response-ability 86
risk/s
   assessment 40, 42, 43, 91, 93
   averse 88, 90, 94
   aversion 88, 116
   benefit assessment 91

emotional   4, 11, 13, 16, 25, 34, 35, 39, 41–3, 50, 81, 90, 96, 97, 101, 108–110, 117
risk-taking   15, 87, 88, 90, 94–6, 98
rules   3, 6, 7, 21, 29–31, 33, 36, 46–8, 51, 69–71, 84, 122, 127, 128, 147
Runswick-Cole, K.   58, 59
Russell, W.   2, 3, 10, 13, 22, 23, 25, 31, 36, 47, 50, 72, 75, 76, 80, 85, 86, 97, 98, 101, 106, 108, 120, 125, 144

Sandseter, E.   89, 95
The Scottish Care Inspectorate   149
screen time   95, 121, 122
Sexton, J.   71
sexual development   133, 134
Smith, K.   47, 50
social model of disability   63, 67
space
    of childhood   70
    for children   70, 72–8, 80, 85, 86
    closed   75, 76, 78, 79
    conceived   80, 83
    inclusive   56, 57, 60, 62, 68, 150
    lived   81, 82
    open   64, 75, 80
    perceived   80, 81, 83

spacetime   13, 49, 80, 82, 83, 109, 112, 117, 134
Spiegel, B.   90
Sturrock, G   10, 66, 75, 103
Sutton-Smith, B.   5, 10, 52, 105–7, 134

Tawil, B.   89, 96, 98, 120
teacher training   42, 43, 49
three frees   131
transgender   136, 138, 140, 147, 148
Triad theory   80

UN Convention on the Rights of the Child   58, 119
Underdown, A.   119
Uprichard, E.   59

value, institutional   47

Ward, C.   72
well-being   4, 6, 53, 57, 91, 98, 108, 119, 120, 123, 124, 129, 130, 142
Wingrave, M.   139
Wood, A.   8, 10, 13, 19, 25, 27, 30, 36, 42, 113, 123, 133–5, 144, 147, 150
Wragg, M.   2, 11, 17, 60, 75, 153